REA

**FRIENDS
OF ACPL**

ALLEN COUNTY PUBLIC LIBRARY

D0563522

How to Get into the
TOP GRADUATE
SCHOOLS

What You Need to Know About Getting into Law, Medical, and Other Ivy League Schools Explained Simply

By David Wilkening

FEB 0 6 2009

THE HUMANE SOCIETY OF THE UNITED STATES ©

The human-animal bond is as old as human history. We cherish our animal companions for their unconditional affection and acceptance. We feel a thrill when we glimpse wild creatures in their natural habitat or in our own backyard.

Unfortunately, the human-animal bond has at times been weakened. Humans have exploited some animal species to the point of extinction.

The Humane Society of the United States makes a difference in the lives of animals here at home and worldwide. The HSUS is dedicated to creating a world where our relationship with animals is guided by compassion. We seek a truly humane society in which animals are respected for their intrinsic value, and where the human-animal bond is strong.

Want to help animals? We have plenty of suggestions. Adopt a pet from a local shelter, join the Humane Society and be a part of our work to help companion animals and wildlife. You will be funding our educational, legislative, investigative, and outreach projects in the U.S. and across the globe.

Or perhaps you would like to make a memorial donation in honor of a pet, friend or relative? You can through our Kindred Spirits program. And if you would like to contribute in a more structured way, our Planned Giving Office has suggestions about estate planning, annuities, and even gifts of stock that avoid capital gains taxes.

Maybe you have land that you would like to preserve as a lasting habitat for wildlife. Our Wildlife Land Trust can help you. Perhaps the land you want to share is a backyard—that's enough. Our Urban Wildlife Sanctuary Program will show you how to create a habitat for your wild neighbors.

So you see, it's easy to help animals. And the HSUS is here to help.

The Humane Society of the United States
2100 L Street NW
Washington, DC 20037
202-452-1100
www.hsus.org

Table of Contents

Foreword

By Eric L. Walters, PhD

The decision to attend graduate school should be a no-brainer. Why? Graduate school enriches both the mind and the pocketbook. Many studies have shown that individuals who have attended graduate school are, on average, happier and wealthier because of the experience. *How To Get Into the Top Graduate Schools* provides a plethora of information on the process of applying to and attending graduate school. If you are considering postgraduate academics, you owe it to yourself to fully understand the commitment you are making to the next two to seven years of your life. David Wilkening's pointers and insider information open a door to a world of opportunity.

When I think back to my decision to enter graduate school, I remember the frustration I experienced without having any resources to consult on how to go about applying to schools. Even with the advent of the Internet and the myriad increase in publishing means, there remains a paucity of sources for instruction on finding, applying to, and entering graduate schools. Compounding the problem is the misconception by many that methods used when applying to undergraduate institutions can be used for postgraduate programs. Applicants who assume the undergraduate method will work when applying to graduate schools are doomed before they even begin. The information in this book comes 17 years too late for me but presents itself as a gift to those currently mulling over the decision of whether to attend graduate school in the future.

Getting into graduate school requires a tremendous amount of preparation and organization. But, being accepted to an Ivy League or top graduate school requires even more effort. The good news is that most applicants are rather naïve and, therefore, it is relatively easy to stand out among the pool of applicants if you have done your homework. Having served on several graduate selection committees, I know from experience that there are certain tricks to getting the attention of a selection committee. This book identifies all facets of the application procedure and gives the reader unique information on what, and what not, to include when preparing a winning application.

How To Get Into the Top Graduate Schools includes varied topics ranging from how to fill out the application forms themselves to knowing yourself to using the proper etiquette in requesting letters of recommendation. Real-world examples and quotes from authorities in their respective fields provide the foundation for successful application strategies. Wilkening even provides a section on what to do if you fail at getting accepted the first time around. His advice on creating a schedule is particularly novel and allows the reader to fully appreciate the scope and timing of the application process. The sooner one starts thinking about the application procedure, the better equipped they will be when the time comes to finalize the submission. The beauty of this book is that it can be used at any stage of the application process.

As someone who has been a member of the academic community at both an Ivy League and a top 10 school, I know that implementing the advice given in *How To Get Into the Top Graduate Schools* will certainly increase your chances over those who are ill-prepared. In the end, there are no guarantees that you will be accepted but you certainly owe it to yourself to arm yourself with the best possible tools for success. If you are serious about graduate school and ready to take the academic plunge then this book should be on your desk.

Graduate life is in itself something you will always treasure. You may have thought that your undergraduate experience was tough but "you ain't seen nothin' yet". It will definitely feel overwhelming at times, challenging you every day. But, in the end, you will be a richer person, having made lifelong friendships among your academic peers, and having had the opportunity to pursue your scholarly passions. Put on your seat belt, turn the page, and get ready for one of life's greatest rides.

Eric L. Walters, PhD
Author of "A Primer On Getting Into Graduate School"
Hastings Natural History Reservation
University of California Berkeley
38601 E Carmel Valley, CA 93294
www.ericlwalters.org/gradschool.htm

Eric received both his BS and MS degrees from the University of Victoria (British Columbia, Canada), where he served on several graduate school selection committees. He obtained his PhD from Florida State University (Tallahassee, FL) and, upon graduating, he accepted a position as a research associate at Dartmouth College (Hanover, NH). Currently, he is employed as a postdoctoral fellow at the University of California Berkeley and has spent the past 14 years helping naïve undergraduates understand how to beat the odds and get accepted to graduate schools.

Preface

What is graduate school? Why is it important to you? What can you expect from it? Perhaps even more fundamental: How can you make sure you are accepted? This book will answer those questions and many others. In simple and basic terms, this vital guide tells you how to get into an Ivy League or top graduate school, which is different from being accepted to Anywhere College, USA.

Whether you are looking into law, medicine, or other graduate schools, this book tells you precisely what you need to know to achieve your goal of being one of the elite. This is your inside scoop on how to make sure you are at the front of the line for admission. It also provides all you need to know about many related topics, including financial help once you are accepted at the school of your dreams, and even some down-to-earth advice on what to do when you receive your acceptance letter.

No one can guarantee that you will get into a top graduate school just through reading this book; but here is a guarantee: If you understand the advice related here, and use good judgment to apply it to your situation, you will greatly improve your chances of being accepted to the school of your choice. In the end, you are the one who determines your success; but here you will find a lot of ideas to help you.

CHAPTER 1

First Things First

What Is Graduate School and Why Do You Want to Be There?

Graduate school is an advanced program of study focused on a particular academic discipline or profession. A graduate school or "grad school" is a school that awards advanced degrees, with the general requirement that students must have earned an undergraduate degree. Many universities award graduate degrees; a graduate school is not necessarily a separate institution. Original research experience is a significant component of graduate studies, including the writing and defense of a thesis or dissertation. The term "graduate school" is primarily used in North America. It also does not usually refer to medical school (advanced students are called "medical students"), and only occasionally refers to law school or business school.

Traditionally, graduate school has been "academic," which means it has been centered on generating original research in a particular discipline. However, today we also have "professional" graduate schools. This type of school emphasizes giving you the skills and knowledge to be a professional, such as a psychologist. There are also graduate schools that combine both traditions.

Perhaps you are wondering, how that is different from undergraduate school? Graduate school requires a higher quality and quantity. Students come to graduate school with the desire to pursue a course of study in a specific discipline or profession. That means there is usually not a lot of room for exploration or elective courses. Additionally, the students' work will be more rigorously evaluated by both faculty and fellow students. Classes tend to be small, and interaction is expected and often necessary in order to excel. Most likely, students will be required to produce some type of original research. These demands are, at times, coupled with a work experience, be it a career-related internship, grading, teaching, or researching.

Unlike undergraduate school, grad school emphasizes an apprenticeship system where student and supervisor work together on research projects. Graduate students take courses as well, but courses are subservient to the aim of developing the skills and expertise required to conduct and publish original research.

Master's degrees are offered in many fields of study. Some are designed to lead to a doctorate degree, while others are the "terminal" degree for a profession, such as Master of Library Science or Master of Business Administration. For full-time students, completing a master's degree usually takes two years. As a part of a master's degree, you may be required to write a master's thesis or complete a fieldwork experience.

Specialist degrees are usually earned in addition to a master's degree. A specialist degree may require coursework, training, or internship experience beyond what was required for a master's degree. This type of degree usually prepares students for professional certification or licensing requirements, such as a high school principal.

Doctorate degrees are the highest degrees possible. They usually require the creation of new knowledge, be it basic or applied. In order to complete a doctorate degree, you will need to be able to conduct independent research. Including the time it takes to write and defend a dissertation, this degree may take anywhere from five to seven years to complete.

More About Why You Should Go

There are various reasons why you should go to graduate school. Remember that a master's degree is serious investment of time, money, and work. Most master's programs take two years to complete. Total costs can run more than $50,000 a year. Even if you take on a loan debt to finance your degree, you may be looking at decades-long repayment. Then, there is the job market itself. In many fields, such as academia, jobs are hard to find.

So before you take the leap to enroll in school, you should have an idea of where your interests are. You should also know something about what grad school life is like and the programs you think you want to study. Have specific ideas on how your interests tie in with the programs you want to study. Take some time to think about it.

When you are considering grad school, you have to think about the differences between higher education and the undergraduate education that precedes it.

There are some significant differences between undergraduate and grad schools. Undergraduate institutions are generally considered to be universities that prepare individuals for greater success in life. The objective is to produce a well-rounded individual who specializes in one area of study, but is also broadly prepared to take on a variety of tasks in life. Most undergraduates work from semester to semester, with little coherency in their curriculum. Once finals are over in the fall, they forget most of the details and begin to focus on those courses they are taking in the spring. Undergraduate education generally focuses on short-term learning through courses of several weeks. Little emphasis is given to integrating the knowledge they have acquired.

In graduate school, you study exclusively in the field of your choice. This means there is no general education requirement, or required courses outside your "major." The emphasis is on learning the material to master your field. You have hurdles to cross — preliminary examinations, oral examinations, thesis writing, and research — but these are not the short-term hurdles of an undergraduate curriculum. They are based upon long-term mastery of your field, and classes are one of the vehicles that help you do this. In addition, you have an objective in graduate school: to contribute to the knowledge in your field. Your short-term goals all have to do with these long-term accomplishments.

Briefly

Noted

After earning his BS degree, Jim took an industry job in Seattle. During his first two years, his salary was increased as he took on more responsibility. But in his third year, he did not receive the promotion he thought he deserved. While discussing it with his supervisor, his boss was called away for a phone call. Jim happened to see the official promotion list left on the desk. It was clear he was passed over by many other less-qualified fellow employees who had an advantage: an M.A. degree. As you might guess, Jim went back to school, earned a master's from Stanford and is now getting regular promotions.

When you attend a major university, you are surrounded by people working on state-of-the-art problems, and you join a team that is specializing in a certain area of study and will work to contribute to this area and this team. It takes some "spin up" to be able to work on these hard problems, but when you begin to contribute, the feeling is highly satisfactory.

At a major university, many people are working on the most interesting problems in their respective fields; that is what they get paid to do. An undergraduate solves problems that illustrate the concepts presented in class; a graduate student works on problems that have national and international significance. Dare we say it: It is fun.

There is also the lifestyle. A university campus is a wonderful place to live and work. You will join a team of researchers and work on interesting problems in a great learning environment. You probably will work long hours; but they will be your hours. Yes, you will not have a lot of money, but the environment, the freedom, the people, and the work make for an enjoyable lifestyle. But the number-one reason is an even more serious one: An advanced degree will translate into more money in your future.

Yes, that is the big reason — compensation. You are making an investment in yourself and your future. Most studies show that people with advanced degrees earn more on average than people with bachelor's degrees. In a recent year, the U. S. Census Bureau found the average person with a bachelor's degree earned just over $40,000. Someone with a master's degree, however, typically earned more than $50,000.

Over a lifetime, a person with a master's degree can earn around $13,000 per year or $500,000 more during their lifetimes than someone with a bachelor's degree, according to the U.S. Census Bureau.

Graduate school admittedly is work. It is not always easy. You should know it does not guarantee you a dream career. But despite the difficulties, there are many compelling reasons to get a degree.

If you want to be a psychologist, social worker, or therapist, you will need an advanced degree. In addition, if you are in those careers, you will need insurance. Increasingly, insurance companies authorize payment only to practitioners who meet educational as well as licensing standards.

There is also the issue of remaining marketable. It is obvious that many jobs do not require an advanced degree, particularly at the entry level. However, it is advantageous when you are trying out for more competitive and desirable positions.

Your master's degree may make a difference between getting the job and being left out. Also, keep in mind that upper levels of your career may require an advanced degree, no matter how smart or competent you are.

Career changes also come up for many people. A graduate degree in hand often gives you greater options if you need or want to change direction later in your career.

Some students argue that they cannot afford to go to graduate school. Perhaps the reverse is true, however — they cannot afford not to go.

Case Study: Abraham Quintanar

"[For] preparing yourself...there is no way to know what to expect from graduate school. Everyone has a different experience. Don't get discouraged. This is part of the learning experience." — Abraham Quintanar, assistant professor of Spanish, Dickinson College

---

And what about the job market itself? If it is bad, you might want to stay in school after your undergraduate days and wait out the job market.

Then again, you might have a love of learning. Or maybe you love the field you are studying. Or your continuing on in school provides welcome intellectual stimulation.

Let us look at personal satisfaction. If you are interested in a specific field of study, be it literature, business, or biology, going to graduate school will let you pursue that field to the limits of current knowledge. Graduate school will help you become an expert in your field.

Briefly

Noted

"Don't let schooling interfere with your education."

Mark Twain

There is also the matter of choosing what you want to do with your life and your work. Graduate school will help there, too. Studies show that more than 80 percent of people who complete graduate degrees are happy with their choice to attend graduate school.

Still another issue is the intangible question of leadership. Want to be a leader? The chances of achieving that are higher if you complete graduate school, experts say. With a graduate degree, you are much more likely to have management responsibilities and more freedom to conduct your own work. That sense of responsibility and freedom can be both challenging and exciting.

There is always the question of timing, however. Should you enroll in graduate school right after college or work for a few years after completing your undergraduate studies? Why go to graduate school right after your B.A.? Your study skills are still sharp, is one reason. Another is you are accustomed to being a student. Also, you have momentum going for you. Remember that some occupations require an advanced degree even for entry-level positions.

But on the other hand, there are reasons for working for a few years before starting grad school. For example, you may better know your own career goals by working in your chosen field for a few years. If you wait, you will likely bring a broader world view to your studies. You will be more mature and able to juggle work and school more adeptly. Perhaps your employer will even pay part or all of your graduate school expenses. You may be on surer financial footing.

And why set your sights for a top school? Let us look at your ambitions: If you are interested in a teaching career, then you will want to get into the most prestigious school you can.

Most people would not disagree that Ivy League and top schools provide a better level of teaching, a better level of social networking, and a signal to future employers that the degree-holder could be worth paying more than average graduates.

What about other fields outside of academia?

Let us leave out the Ivy and the top school question for a minute and take a look at common sense. As you might imagine, when corporate recruiters look at first-time job seekers, they look first at graduates from the top-tier schools. Common sense also tells us there is such a thing as what some call "the good old boy network." Like it or not, we live in a real world where a tight alumni network helps offer opportunities for those well-paying jobs. It is human nature to want to surround ourselves with others who may share common college experiences.

It is conventional wisdom that dropping names can often get you far in life. Saying you attended a prestigious university during job interviews is no different.

And it is the perception of being a more "run-of-the-mill" school that is a lingering problem. Even admissions to graduate schools often reflect a bias toward Ivy League-educated students: nearly one-third of Harvard Law School is composed of students who received an undergraduate degree from one of the eight Ivy League schools (Brown, Columbia, Cornell, Dartmouth, Harvard, Pennsylvania, Princeton, and Yale).

Irrespective of the training students receive at the top-ranked colleges, a degree from Harvard, Yale, or Princeton carries significant value for first-time job seekers, and perhaps even for promotions thereafter. Ask recruiters who unabashedly state that they have discrepant thresholds for interviewing candidates based on their school. Nicholas Lehmann said in a PBS Frontline interview, "a good school puts you in the way of more opportunity."

And what about sheer enjoyment or pleasure? Consider what *Crimson* (the school newspaper) called "Harvard's most successful dropout." This was at a graduating class of his alma mater, Harvard, last year:

"What I remember above all about Harvard was being in the midst of so much energy and intelligence. It could be exhilarating, intimidating, sometimes even discouraging, but always challenging. It was an amazing privilege — and though I left early, I was transformed by my years at Harvard, the friendships I made, and the ideas I worked on."

And more: "Harvard was just a phenomenal experience for me. Academic life was fascinating. I used to sit in on lots of classes I had not even signed up for. And dorm life was terrific. There were always lots of people in my dorm room late at night discussing things, because everyone knew I did not worry about getting up in the morning."

The speaker was Bill Gates, of course.

Truths and Myths About Graduate School

There are a lot of truths and myths about getting into a top or Ivy League grad school. Gaining admission to the nation's top graduate schools is one of the most competitive and least understood processes in education today. However, the value placed on receiving a prestigious university education over the past decade has increased dramatically. More students than ever are looking to attend the nation's elite schools. At the same time, the appeal and reach of the Ivy League has broadened to attract international students.

Perhaps the most persistent misunderstanding is that graduates with excellent grades are the first to be accepted. Many find it hard to believe that this is not the case at all. The applicants with the best grades do not get accepted first. Like life itself, the process of getting into a graduate school is not a fair one. You might have excellent grades, but keep in mind there are no guarantees of acceptance, and remember that the process for graduate school admission decisions is different from undergraduate admissions.

It is easy to see why students routinely assume that admission to graduate school depends in large part on good grades. After all, that is one of the main qualifications for admission to many undergraduate programs. No wonder students are under this mistaken notion.

No one would disagree that outstanding grades will help get you accepted. However, if you are only an average or slightly above-average student, you can also be accepted. Why? Because of the ways that students are taught and evaluated in graduate school. Students who doubt they can get in because their grades are not good enough are often simply wrong.

There have been studies that found correlations between undergraduate GPAs (grade point average) and graduate school success in some disciplines. However, those analyses typically involved large groups of students. Many faculty members argue that the correlation is not there when considering only students in individual programs. Even in disciplines where there are stronger relations between undergraduate and graduate grades, no one can deny there are many exceptions.

Another common misconception is that graduate school programs delve deeply into a narrow range of subject matter. Research and skills development are usually the focus. You will be too busy learning useful things to worry about sitting in a classroom for hours on end.

You should keep in mind that the graduate school process starts the same as the undergraduate process. You fill out admission forms and submit your grades. After that, the process is different. Your application is passed on to individual faculty members identified as potential supervisors. It is crucial to understand that the primary decision maker will be an individual faculty member, with decisions sometimes reviewed by a small committee of faculty members.

In a given year, a faculty member may or may not consider any applications. If the faculty member is in the market or wants new students, he or she will be looking for standouts, applicants who have what it takes to succeed. By accepting a student, a faculty member is making a serious commitment in time and resources. If the student does well, everyone benefits; but if the student fails, the faculty member's career could suffer. You have to believe faculty members take this to heart.

There are a lot of other myths and misunderstandings about graduate school. For example, some think it is just like being an undergraduate, only harder. Graduate school is a mix of many things. As a student, you will be taking classes for the first couple of years. You will also be designing and implementing experiments and you may also be asked to teach. At the same time, you will be asked to focus on your specific research questions intensely and independently. You will be expected to understand the field, and do the reading that is necessary for you to do that. The positive aspect of all this is that you set your own schedule. The negative is that you have to be disciplined to stick to this schedule. But as a bonus, being a full-time student lets you more easily enjoy the camaraderie of other students.

Another misconception is that some students believe they cannot afford graduate school. In fact, there are many ways to pay for your education. There are fellowships, scholarships, teaching assistantships, and research assistantships. There will almost certainly be some avenues of financial support if you attend school full-time. It is a good investment to take out a loan to get a master's degree.

Still another myth is that if you earn a master's or a doctoral degree and do not go into academia, you will be overqualified and unable to find a job. While the United States is outsourcing many jobs that do not require higher education, some large companies are hiring more than half of their new employees with graduate degrees.

Another myth on the negative side is that having a graduate degree in and of itself will put you on the fast track for promotion. Your work ethic, your relationship with your boss, and what you produce are important elements, with or without an M.A. Think about what it will mean to have a degree from a top university. Not surprisingly, many students looking for a master's degree do not know where to begin.

Students also should be aware of the basic nature of graduate school. Many incorrectly think it is just an extension of earlier school. The best comparison is the difference between high school and college. It comes as a shock to many students to find college much less structured than high school. Similarly, graduate students have much the same reaction as they make the transition from undergraduate life.

A typical full-time course load is nine hours. You will spend less time in class in graduate school than as an undergraduate. But the demands now are much greater than those of an undergraduate. Students might spend three or four hours of preparation for every hour in class. Standards are higher as well. If you are getting a C, forget it; this is usually not a passing grade in graduate school. There are generally fewer exams and due dates. And one thing is for sure: It is far easier to yield to an urge to procrastinate.

A master's student typically completes a specified set of courses in the first year or so, and then spends time working on a research project with a faculty member. The completed project is written up as a thesis, and the candidate gives a talk to a group of three or four faculty members and defends the work. The entire process may take two years, perhaps three. Some schools allow a written exam plus a scholarly paper to substitute for the research project.

The Ph.D. student follows a similar track, perhaps taking

some required courses and a written exam. There may be a foreign language exam as well. Before research is begun, however, there is usually an oral exam during which the candidate presents the research idea and is questioned about the necessary background knowledge. The student then completes the thesis research, writes it up, and has an oral defense. The entire process may take five years of graduate study or three years beyond the master's degree.

A side word here: if you want to be a college professor, you might wonder if it is worth the time and trouble to get a Ph.D. at a time when universities are cutting back on their hiring and are even closing academic departments. The answer is yes, at least if you are willing to be flexible about your ultimate position. There is a strong and continuing demand for good, knowledgeable people with expertise, even in times of downsizing.

Briefly

Noted

Take the example of Alex. He has a doctorate in economics and was a professor in Tennessee. Burned out with teaching, he tried Wall Street, where he is now an authority on predicting which technical stocks are good investments.

Is It Affordable?

The question of whether or not you can afford to attend a top graduate school varies, of course. A crucial task is to look at the costs of the various programs and determine what financial aid is possible at different schools. Keep in mind that most graduate programs offer fellowships for teaching or for being research assistants. These can reduce your expenses.

So take a look at what it will cost. These are the types of expenses you will need to consider:

- Tuition

- Housing

- Books

- Fees

- Health insurance (if any)

- Travel and transportation, such as parking and auto insurance

- Computer, art supplies, or other necessary equipment

- Child care, if applicable

Now that you have an idea what it will cost you, look at your own financial situation. Do you have a family member who will help subsidize you? Can you work part-time? Can you take out loans?

Some of your grad school money will come from sources

you control, such as loans, outside jobs, savings, and family members. Everything else, however, comes from one of two sources: the first source is internal funding or money that is controlled by the university; the second source is money from external sources, such as fellowships.

You will find that universities have a large number of aid sources, but they often are not in one central location. You can look first in your own department or college, and then try the overall Financial Aid Office. In addition, there are often Graduate Colleges that deal with aid just for graduate programs.

Financial aid through the university is usually in the form of fellowships, other assistantships, work-study programs, and student loans. Generally, you have to apply for loans to the Financial Aid Office.

Some external fellowships are funded by the government or by foundations, but these often require a nomination from your program or the university. You can apply for some external fellowships independently; but to be successful, you will need recommendations from your departments. These are often not easy to get before you start the school year.

The key to graduate school has a common thread with other endeavors: start early, as early as you possibly can. The most common problems for would-be graduate students worried about money are a lack of understanding of the full range of funding sources and insufficient or late planning. There is a great variety of ways to fund your education, but unless you start looking at them early, you are going to miss some of the best opportunities. Take a look at this critical area at least a year before you expect to apply for graduate school.

Remember that private and government scholarship competitions have application deadlines at various times throughout the year. Remember also that many scholarships and other award programs administered by universities or departments have application deadlines before the graduate program application deadlines.

Your Chances of Getting In

If anybody tells you it is easy to get into a top graduate school, ignore their advice. It is not easy; but it is not impossible, either.

Admittance rates for the top graduate schools generally are in the 10 to 15 percent range. Getting accepted depends, of course, on the competition and the number of applicants.

Myriad factors make it difficult to devise a formula that can account for the evaluation of the various skills and potentials of highly qualified individuals. That is the goal of the admissions office, which guides its judgment according to the educational and philosophical goals of the school. But one element is certain: there are more applicants each year. And it becomes more difficult all the time.

Case Study: Eran Magen

Israeli-born Eran Magen has a short version of how to get into graduate school: "All I had was a B.A. with a very unexciting average. No contacts, no research experience. Nothing. I had serious doubts I could do it. I put work into it for about a year, while working to support myself. I did it. And so can anyone, including you." She attended Stanford.

Credit: Eran Magen, **http://www.HowIGotIntoStanford.com**

Admissions officers always take a close look at your GPA. Beyond that, it is good to have at least some background in psychology and some exposure to statistics. If you plan to go on after your M.A. degree to get a doctorate, you should be aware that is an even more difficult prospect. Some doctoral programs accept less than 2 percent, which is about the lowest rate of any graduate program in any discipline.

Remember, there is more to getting in than grades. Your admissions essay, teacher recommendations, application forms, activity descriptions, extracurricular involvement, talents, achievements and personal interviews are also important.

To have the best chance, you will need to focus on

learning everything you can about the admissions process. You will need to find out what works and what does not. In particular, look at your own activities and focus on those. If science is your passion, you should find ways of showing it to the college. If business excites you, consider focusing on that. If you are involved in a number of activities outside of class, be sure to include them in your dealings with admission officials. Also, be sure to start early on your applications. It can take several months to write a good essay and get it just right.

In reading this book, you will start to understand the admission process and also the administrators or gatekeepers who either will either accept or reject your application. You probably have not given much thought to administrators or what they are like — their particular natures and desires. That is understandable, after all, because you are focusing on the entire admission process. But keep in mind that admissions officers have personalities, too, and if you understand what makes them tick, you increase your chances of convincing them of your desirability as a student.

Admissions officers usually come in two types. The first group often involves talented recent college graduates. They tend to be bright and are often interested in education. They are using this job as a stepping-stone to move into teaching or other areas. As a group, they are still in touch with students. They also have a tendency to take more risks. The second group includes people from all walks of life who have been doing this kind of work for a long time. They may be more out of touch with actual students. They probably did not come from an Ivy League or top college, because if they did, they would have better jobs. This group is going to have a harder time recognizing talented applicants. The likelihood is that the admission officer reading your application is the type who has been there a long time.

Your understanding after completing this book will help you find ways of dealing with the personality of the admissions people who hold your fate in their hands. You will see how telling the truth but emphasizing the positive and never hiding behind a false sense of modesty is the starting point in how to deal with your admissions officer.

How This Book Will Help You Get Accepted

No one can ever guarantee success in getting accepted at the level of Ivy League or a top graduate school, nor can they promise you success in getting your degree. But if you study what is in this book, and master its advice, the odds of your success will greatly increase.

This book starts with the basics, such as showing you how to evaluate yourself and where you fit in with the graduate school profile. Following that, all aspects of graduate life are covered.

If you look at the chapters of this book, you will see

they cover all the bases. You will find out what graduate school is like. You will learn how to get the information you need. You will find help in selecting and evaluating the right programs for you. The best sources of financial aid will be found in this book. It will also tell you how your writing can help you gain entrance to the graduate school of your choice.

Good references are also important, particularly if you are not in the top grade levels and do not have the highest test results. This book will give you instruction on how to get a good reference.

What are admissions officials looking for? With insight from this book, you will find the answers to that question as well. As you may or may not know, if you read through any school's history of admission, you will find a consistent message: the goal is to create 21st-century leaders.

You will learn how to maximize certain characteristics of all admissions offices. You will find many tips to enhance your chances of getting a positive response from admissions officers. For example, you should research schools that focus their marketing efforts on areas of study that match your own academic interests. These schools may be looking to increase enrollments in these majors.

You will also find a lot of similar information you can use. University administrators in nonacademic life routinely lobby admissions officials to admit more candidates interested in an array of social, cultural, and extracurricular activities. The music or orchestra director, for example, might want more cellists in any given year. The athletic director, on the other hand, might stress the role of athletes. Knowing information such as this greatly enhances your chances of acceptance.

And what about once you get in? The book will tell you how to handle that as well.

Financial aid should also be considered. Unless you are independently wealthy, you will need some advice on how to pay your way (and perhaps support yourself) while you are in graduate school.

But that is only the beginning, because to succeed, you have to do your homework. As part of that procedure, you will learn new skills, such as how to write essays and solicit letters from others that will further your chances of acceptance. So if your grades are not the best or your test scores are not among the highest in the nation, you do not have to accept the notion that the best schools will not take you. By conventional standards, you might not expect to be accepted by the best grad schools, but this book provides you with inside information on how to maximize the talents you have at your disposal. Information in this book will show you how to overcome possible handicaps such as lower grades.

For example, you will see how to make your application stand out among the many others. You will quickly see that you need to acquire all the knowledge you can about graduate school. In a sense, getting into graduate school has some similarities to a lawyer getting ready to go to court. Your lawyer wants to present the best case. So do you, whether that means perfectly filling out the applications, preparing for a critical personal interview, or knowing how to write convincing reference letters. You want to make it easy for the admissions committee to say yes. You want to give them the best case you can mount.

At its most basic, this book is your indispensable guide to getting in, staying in, and getting out of graduate school. If that is your goal, turn the page.

CHAPTER 2

Life as a Graduate Student

Pretend, for a minute, that you are in graduate school. You have made it to an Ivy League or top graduate school. What is your life like these days?

You will need to think more than ever about money. That is a good place to start. If your graduate school offer contains financial aid, take a close look. Review your finances. You do not want any unpleasant surprises down the road such as an inability to afford your apartment. Perhaps you will have to make some adjustments in your new life as a graduate student. For example, you needed a car before because you had to drive, but now you might get by without that added expense. Look at alternatives.

You need a place to live as you are starting school in the fall. You should find this several months before you start your school work. Once school is in session, there will be far fewer housing options. Help is available here, however. There may be a university office that will help you, or you can try the Dean of Students office.

You should also see the graduate advisor. He or she can help you design your program. Even before meeting with him or her, you should have some idea of where you want to go.

Your university will have an orientation program for new students. Consider it a not-to-be-missed event. Ask questions. Be sure you understand things such as whether you will be teaching as part of your course work or whether you will be required to take on other jobs. As school starts, everyone is busy. Things can be confusing. So take the time to make sure you understand what is going on.

Check whether or not courses you have taken as an undergraduate might be counted for graduate credit. This happens more than you might expect.

Briefly

Noted

"When I was an undergraduate, I always felt invisible, lost in large classrooms. But in graduate school, everyone talked to me — students and instructors. Many students became good friends."

Anonymous student

Graduate school is an unstructured environment in most cases, but you will certainly be reading a lot of technical papers and reports to become familiar with your field. You may find yourself spending more than half of your time reading, especially when you start school. This is normal. It is also normal to be overwhelmed at first by the amount of reading you think is necessary. Try to keep in mind that it is impossible to read everything that might be relevant. Instead, try reading selectively.

Your instructors will vary in their interests and abilities. Speculation about them will be widespread. Talking to other students will help you judge the faculty, but whatever you think of them, you should interact in various ways. It is obvious that some instructors are more generous with their time than others. But most departments have seminars or special lectures for all faculty members. There are social events afterwards. Be on the lookout for encounters that allow you to get to know the faculty. You want your professors to get to know you for better grades, but also for networking in the future. At some point, no matter what you do, you will need references for a fellowship or an assistantship. Getting to know the faculty will pay off in the future, especially when you want a letter of recommendation from a professor.

Briefly

Noted

"It's not the smartest people who get the jobs, it's the people with connections that get jobs. You have to get in with a professor that has some prestige in the field."

Anonymous student

One of the factors you will quickly understand in graduate school is that you better be self-motivated and ambitious. Unlike when you were an undergrad, you will not be spoon-fed information. You will have to find much of the relevant knowledge on your own. You will be teaching, training, and supervising yourself. The faculty is mostly to keep you on track.

You also will need self-confidence, because you will be expected to speak out in class and express your ideas. Not only that, but you should be able to challenge and test the ideas of others. If you are looking further down the road toward getting a doctorate, you should be aware that this can be a five- to ten-year process. It is a much more complicated program than a master's. Ph.D. programs vary, but most will test your knowledge over broad areas in your field. A second type is usually narrower and deeper. It covers the area where you will write your dissertation.

Knowing what you want to do and being self-confident is just about everyone's prescription for success. This book will remind you that, once you are accepted, you become a member of the "program." A department may ask you to take extra courses. In subtle ways, you will see the need to submit to some authority at your school. Once professors see that you are willing to go along, they will feel comfortable with you as a member of the group.

Briefly

Noted

Grad student Samuel Matheson was accepted at an Ivy League school and given an assistantship, but when he talked to his advisor, he demanded credit for a few previous classes he took. Within a few weeks, his acceptance was rescinded. He was a good example of why authority sometimes has to be accepted.

A particularly annoying task when starting graduate school is finding out the specific requirements. This is in contrast to undergraduate work where what is needed is spelled out in catalogues. This is not always the case in grad school, so you will need to make an effort on your own to determine what is needed.

It is also a good idea during your first year to make up a schedule of courses, examinations, and thesis requirements. Then take up this list with your advisor to see if it is practical. Can you do it all? And did you miss anything? You will almost certainly have to change your plan, but at least you have a starting point.

You are on the way to that degree, but you will quickly find that "gentlemanly" Cs as an undergraduate do not work here. Bs are permitted, but are not good. You should work hard enough to get As throughout your graduate school career.

It is also important to find your thesis director or advisor early. Some experts say this is the most important decision after your choice of program. Why? Because you are bound to have a lot of questions and there is inevitably some confusion for some students. In addition, your advisor can help if you need income from assistantships or a teaching job. A good advisor is defined at its simplest as someone who can help you in every way perform at your best as a student. Fellow students can give you advice on choosing a career.

Your career as a graduate student, you will find, tends to fall into separate sections. The first is the beginning, when you find a working title and supervisor. You also get an idea of what you will be looking for and how you will tackle the subject. You will do a literature survey and decide on your own methodology, which has a lot of variations.

Section two is when you analyze the data and write your report. You will find it is a good idea to start writing as the data comes in and not wait until you have a mountain of stuff on paper or in computer files. In section three, you will be writing a draft of each chapter and submitting it to your supervisor for comments and approval. It is usually best to do this one chapter at a time.

You should know that many grad students find loneliness is a problem. The undergraduates have plenty of friends from ongoing courses, but research can be a solitary activity. There may be few other graduate students around working on things that interest you. Universities have structures in place that take care of undergrads and staff, but there are relatively few organized ways of supporting the interests of postgraduates.

Do not let that get you down, however. If you are feeling lonely, go out and make friends. Join a society or a club or two. Join the postgraduate society, if there is one. If one does not exist, consider setting one up to look after the interests of those important but often overlooked members of the university.

How the Selection Process Works

One of the biggest problems many graduate students face is the issue of the gatekeeper, otherwise known as the admissions office. What criteria do they use when deciding whom to let in? Students rarely seem to understand how this process works, so how can they successfully go through procedures they do not understand? They cannot, of course.

There are other criteria in addition to grades that will make your application a success. Even if you have excellent grades, you might not get accepted because you fall short in other areas of determining acceptance.

Graduate acceptance school systems differ, but most have some common elements. No matter where you apply, there are four main factors:

1. Undergraduate GPA

2. Standardized test scores

3. Letters of recommendation

4. Various personal statements

Let us take a closer look at each of these elements.

Obviously, you want your GPA to be as high as possible. If your GPA is borderline, you may benefit from someone reading your transcript course by course. There may be some subject areas where you had problems. Or there may be personal reasons for a lower GPA, such as family or financial difficulties. Keep in mind that the GPA of applicants who have just completed their undergraduate work is almost always given more weight than applicants who return to school after an absence of several years.

The GRE test is typically required for entrance into graduate school. Some schools require taking additional GRE tests, particularly in psychology and the sciences. The GRE General Test is available only as a computer adaptive test. The computer chooses questions for you based on how well you are doing. The GRE General Test measures your knowledge and skills in three areas: verbal, quantitative, and analytical writing. Your GPA generally carries more weight because there is a difference of opinion about the value of tests. The best advice is if you are applying to graduate school within two years of undergraduate courses, take the GRE soon. Studies show that performance on standardized tests declines with each year you are out of school. So get the test out of the way as soon as possible.

Briefly

Noted

"Why do I have to pass another test?" is a common question of students who have proven themselves successful but are returning to graduate school.

It might surprise you, but letters of recommendation can rank high on an admissions committee's list of evaluation criteria. Indeed, they can rank in the top three evaluation elements, along with GPA and GRE scores. Most programs require three letters of recommendation. Your personal statement is another factor that is perhaps less important, but should be as original and interesting as you can make it. It should also be honest and clear, and portray you at your best.

In most universities, the faculty or a school of graduate studies implements administration policies. Often the faculty or school plays only a minor role in the selection process beyond establishing minimum grade requirements or perhaps some other standards that apply to all of the graduate programs. The selection itself is often done by faculty members in the specific department where you are applying.

Many programs have an admissions committee, which is often referred to as a selection committee. They generally include a few faculty members who meet each year after the application deadline to pour over a pile of applications. Most programs also have a graduate program director, who is also on the admissions committee.

The general aim of most admissions committees is to provide a rating of applicants. Ultimately, the rating helps determine who is accepted. The entire process has many elements that include facets of the overall application package. This process often involves eliminating some of the lower-timeranking applicants.

Once your application file is complete, it might sit among a pile of other files for weeks. In some programs (particularly those where students do not study and train under a single faculty member), the admissions committee makes the final decision to accept or reject.

In most doctoral programs, and in master's programs that have a research thesis, students do their work under the supervision of a sponsoring faculty member. That member is known as a graduate supervisor.

After all the files are collected, the admissions committee takes a look. Acceptable candidates are distributed to the faculty members whom applicants have indicated they want as their graduate supervisor. These individual faculty members make the decision of who is accepted or denied.

An individual professor might have five, ten, or even a dozen students applying to do work under his or her supervision. Many faculty members will still accept applicants despite a poor rating from the admissions committee. Why? They might be impressed by some aspect of the applicant that outweighs the admissions committee. Some faculty members do not put as much reliance on grades of standardized test scores, or perhaps low rankings there are outweighed in the professor's mind by other personality traits. So whatever your grades and test scores, this is an area where aspiring graduate students can greatly increase their acceptance chances by creatively using the system.

In many programs, a faculty member's consent or desire to serve as an applicant's supervisor is among the main reasons for success. It behooves an applicant to find ways (which will be detailed here) of convincing faculty members that it is in their own best interest to take you as a student.

The old cliché "publish or perish" is still critical in modern-day universities. The output of many professors depends on a lot of presenting or publishing of their work. So it is easy to see why they would want graduate students who enhance their own self-interest.

Professors are looking to bring the most promising people into their own projects. This eliminates any notion that a selection process is above board, fair, and impartial. It is not. Neither is life itself.

One of the first concerns of an admissions committee is if an applicant's interests match the program's own goals. It is easy to tell when this is not the case. Much harder, at least for the student, is to figure out how to fit in with the particular program.

After determining that the applicant's intentions match the program, the admissions committee considers other elements. Here, the applicants clearly want to demonstrate how they are the "perfect match." One way to do this is for students in scientific fields, such as chemistry, to participate in original research while they are still undergraduates.

There is also the question of character and personality. Admissions committees have a vested interest in ensuring they only allow people of character to get into their programs. They want students who are mature, polite, and generally agreeable. Faculty and admissions committee members realize they will be spending many hours with these students, so they must have winning personalities. Students underestimate this aspect of the selection process at their peril.

Students also forget something else that appears obvious to an objective observer: The person who agrees to supervise your graduate studies wants something in return. Graduate supervisors are people, too.

While admissions decisions are necessarily subjective to some degree and only represent qualitative judgments about your likely success in graduate school, there are ways for students to show why they will be a success.

1. Make sure that you present your strongest case. Do not even let the admissions committee think about saying no. If you are prepared and have all the necessary prerequisites, you will show the

admissions committee that you are committed and really want the degree.

2. Make sure that you meet your deadlines. With various deadlines, it may be easy to get confused, but if you really want the degree, you will make sure to meet the deadlines. Give yourself plenty of time to meet each deadline. It may take several weeks for your transcript requests to be processed, so make sure to do it ahead of time. Whether or not you meet your deadlines may be whether or not you are accepted.

Take a closer look. Let us say you are applying to enter Harvard's History of American Civilization program.

The application fee is negligible, only $90. The procedure is to sign up with Harvard, which then welcomes you to complete the first step. Online instruction are simple and direct; some even have a self-rating asking readers to evaluate the questions. Your first application form includes the usual data, such as name, address, and citizenship information. Other forms include your essay, which is part of your "statement of purpose," a dean's letter, a list of programs, answers to the most commonly asked questions, information on costs/financial residence requirements, financial aid instructions, and deadline information.

The Harvard College Admissions Office estimates it will cost students more than $51,000 a year to cover minimal educational and living expenses. If students do not apply for financial aid, they must be able to prove they have sufficient funds to meet that standard.

One of the most commonly asked questions involves application deadlines. Harvard has four different deadlines, depending on the type of graduate school.

The school accepts about 11 percent of the applicants. Graduate class size is about 700. Students must have an impressive undergraduate record.

Students need faculty recommendations, and they will also need to write a statement of purpose. These are carefully considered for admission. Students may also want to submit research papers and other original works to be evaluated.

Depending on the degree sought, students will need to take the GRE, Graduate Record Exam. Some programs may require individual GRE Subject Test scores, while other programs may want students to take the GMAT, Graduate Management Admission Test. Students may also find that they need specific undergraduate courses, to know certain languages, or to have quantitative expertise.

Simplified Components of Graduate School Applications

You might think this is as simplistic as you can get: fill out a form with your name, address, experience, and so on. You would be wrong to dismiss these seemingly innocuous forms. And you should know that students make many mistakes when it comes to "simply filling out a form."

Many students think, for example, this is a matter of minutes or a couple of hours. They grossly underestimate the time that should be spent here. Students are also sometimes careless and do not follow instructions. It is impossible to remind students enough times that they need to always follow instructions. And do not be messy, inaccurate, or even worse, incomplete when filling out the forms. The application form will make an impression. It is up to you whether it will be negative or positive.

You may not believe these forms are important, but admissions committees think differently, and it is easy to make simple mistakes that detract from your overall efforts.

Briefly

"It's just an application form, isn't it?"

Anonymous student

Noted

Application forms almost always have several forms. There are also return envelopes, conformation-or-receipt forms, and various other items. There may be multiple addresses and different deadlines. Application forms are all different, but they should help you keep track of your procedures.

Most graduate school applications have two forms: one for the department where you are applying, and another used for all the graduate programs at the university. Make sure you are sending each form to the right place.

It is a good idea to make two copies of each form. You can practice on one version. If it sounds like a lot of work to fill out a form, perhaps it is; but hopefully you are convinced now that this is an important exercise. It is also important when practicing that you figure out how to make everything fit into the available spaces. Some forms provide small spaces.

Take your time practicing. Plan to take a couple of days instead of hours. Once you are satisfied, you can do the real thing.

Usually, the overall application forms include your statement, an essay, or letter telling about yourself. Applications also normally contain transcripts of your undergraduate and other courses sent directly by the colleges with the institution's official seal. Copies made by you are probably not acceptable. The application form includes letters of recommendation. Graduate or professional examination scores are also part of the process. Do not forget to pay your application fee. That sounds simple, but many students make that mistake.

Your letters of recommendation are important. The best ones, in this case, are from undergraduate professors, other professors, professionals who have supervised you, and employers. If you cannot find professors, you can also use colleagues or graduate students in your field.

The letters are important because they vouch for your ability to study at the graduate level. Professors are the ideal source for these claims because they can apply your talents directly to the particular graduate school. Some programs even stipulate that some letters come from your professors. Here is some good advice: If you have been lingering at the back of the class, get more upfront and make eye contact with your professor. It is good if you can find letters of recommendation from famous or well-known figures in your field, but usually that is not possible. Truly impressive recommendations coming from those who know you personally and have seen the good work you do are fine substitutes for the famous. After an application season that may involve reading three letters from hundreds of applicants, the evaluator is aware of how well someone knows you.

Your personal statement is another area where you will need to take time. There are two goals here: be persuasive and be personal. Persuasive is convincing the admissions committee that you are the right person for the school. Your statement should tell why you fit, but also why you are applying for this particular program.

Making your letter personal involves both honesty and

setting yourself apart from the other applicants. Honesty is something you should already know about and should come naturally to you. But think about your statement of purpose: many are dull and tend not to touch on real issues. Students often have a reticence to opening up their thoughts and feelings. You can squeeze all personality out of your letters, making them dull and listless, or you can show the type of attractive person you are.

Your letter should strike a balance between the persuasive and the personal. Consider that the program also helps decide that balance. In science-related fields, for example, you might want to lean toward persuasive. You might want to highlight your clinical experience and practical interests. In arts and literature, there is usually more room for creativity. You can give the committee more of a window on the workings of your own particular mind.

What else goes in a personal statement? It is all fair game. You might want to include childhood experiences and your social and cultural background, for example. What makes you tick? Obviously, you will need to do some thinking here.

Most students seem not to realize that writing is not the right word. It is re-writing that counts. Do not send out a first draft. Go back and make changes in what you have written. Repeat this as many times as is necessary until you know it is right.

Briefly

Noted

"You never finish writing. You just quit."

Poet and educator Donald Hall

Do not forget something. That is, try to respond to every question and line item. Skipping items makes it look like, at best, you are careless, and at worst, that you are avoiding certain questions. If something is not clear, ask. Never guess.

Make it easy for the admissions committee by putting all the forms in the right order. That makes it easier for them to compare different applicants, and since your application has been done with great care, that comparison will make you look good.

Double-check to make sure everything is complete and accurate before you send off your application forms. It is important to send this in as error-free and complete as possible.

Sloppiness is the most common mistake with bad spelling and grammatical errors. The solution: proofread carefully.

In addition to helping you get into graduate school, there is another important element to your getting the application forms right. If your forms help you get a fellowship, a teaching assistantship, or a tuition waiver, this can mean $50,000 to a master's degree student.

What You Should Know When Choosing a School

You know your goal: get into an Ivy League or other top graduate school. But you have to determine which one.

It often depends on what program you are looking at. Journalists might want to consider Columbia, while would-be lawyers might be more inclined to consider Harvard. It all depends.

Let us start with what are known as the original Ivy League universities.

- Harvard University, established in 1636, is the oldest institution for higher learning in the United States, and offers 40 professional and graduate schools. The Harvard Law School is the nation's oldest continuously operating law school. Perhaps no school in the nation is more prestigious.

- For a smaller school, Brown University offers 38 master's programs and 34 Ph.D. programs. The School of Medicine has gained national recognition for its family and primary care expertise.

- Columbia University is perhaps best known for its Graduate School of Journalism, recognized as one of the best (if not *the* best) in the country.

- Cornell University in Ithaca, New York, offers some graduate programs in New York City. Cornell came up with the nation's first university degree in veterinary medicine, but it is also known for its electrical engineering programs. The school offered the first doctorates in that field, as well as industrial engineering.

- Dartmouth College is smaller and somewhat limited since it offers only 16 graduate programs in the arts and sciences. It also offers the nation's first graduate management school. With an enrollment of only 5,500, the school prides itself on providing a small, intimate atmosphere.

- Princeton University has graduate programs in the humanities, social sciences, natural sciences, engineering, architecture, public affairs, and urban and regional planning. The college does not have graduate programs in business, education, law, medicine, or theology.

- The University of Pennsylvania has only a dozen graduate programs. The Wharton School is the world's first collegiate business school.

- Three-hundred-year-old Yale University has a Graduate School of Arts and Sciences and ten renowned professional schools. The Yale

University School of Medicine is considered a leading center for biomedical research, education and advanced healthcare.

Since you are looking at the top schools, you could simply pick the top ten in your particular field. Students should also be aware of what qualities were used to establish a program's ranking. They should also consider what resources they will find if they choose from the best.

One criteria that may play an important role in the decision of which graduate program is right for you may be geography, Is the program is located in an area of the state or country in which you want to live? Be aware that you will be living in this area for an average of two to six years or more, depending on whether you are seeking a master's degree or Ph.D. Furthermore, your first jobs after graduate school may be in the immediate area.

Briefly

Noted

When looking at graduate schools, consider where you want to live, suggests Caleb John Clark, who has several master's degrees. "No one told me this one. After you graduate, work will probably be easiest to find close to school because your professors, alumni, internships, and the school's reputation are concentrated there," he says.

Perhaps the first thing to do when evaluating where you want to go is to look inwards. What kind of career are you looking for?

Even the top schools have programs that are geared for different areas. For example, a program in economics might offer specific areas of expertise such as econometrics, microeconomics, or economic development. Programs also vary in their flexibility.

That means you need to have some idea of what kind of career objective you have for attending graduate school. Your library and the Internet are helpful, but you can also talk to professors, career counselors, and others.

It may seem like a lot of work to narrow your search, and it is, but by taking the time to make the right decision, you are ensuring a better future.

Know yourself is always good advice. If you want to go back to school just to get your graduate degree, you are not the only one. While it is true that most people know what they want to go back to school for before they begin their search for the right program, there are people out there who begin their search for no other reason than the nebulous yearning they have to go back to school to earn a graduate degree in something. This is more common now than it ever has been before.

For years, a bachelor's degree was enough to make people stand out from the crowd; now, however, a bachelor's is often seen merely as a stepping stone along a much longer path that includes graduate school. In other words, as more and more people go to college, a graduate degree is increasingly necessary for professional advancement in certain fields.

If you are a member of the second group, your best bet is to simply research the possible degrees you can earn in all the fields that interest you. Then compare them with the list you have made (you have made a list, right?) of all the possible careers that appeal to you. Beyond this, it is up to you to figure out what you want to do. If, however, you are a member of the first group, then your first step should be to ask yourself the following three questions:

- Where do I want to go to school?

- Is there a specific aspect of a field that interests me most?

- What degree do I want to earn?

This will help you narrow down your field.

This issue also forces you to deal with how serious you are about pursuing a graduate degree. After all, college was the time to dabble in a number of different areas of study. Graduate school is when you focus on one specific area and make the most of your education in it. And the truth is that, in many fields, from law to medicine to academics, you may have to move to a city or town that you are not in love with to take the first step along the road to professional success. If you are unwilling to move for school, you may want to reconsider how serious you are about pursuing your goals.

Of course, sometimes it is just not possible to move far

away. Family obligations, professional necessities — all kinds of factors can affect your ability to move. And there is absolutely nothing wrong with this. Either way, if you can narrow down your geographic preferences, you will have a much smaller pool of schools from which to choose. And that, after all, is the goal of this process.

Graduate students, unlike undergrads, generally become experts in a specific aspect of their chosen field. If you earn a degree in political science, for example, you will have focused on and become an expert in a specific aspect of that field, whether it is the political history of the Middle East, or the post-Soviet economic development of the Baltic Republics, or something entirely different.

Many schools offer graduate degrees in political science, but only a few of them will specialize in the specific aspects of the field that interest you most. Compile a comprehensive list of schools that fit the academic bill (as well as the geographic one), and proceed from there.

There are two basic graduate degrees you can pursue outside of attending professional schools for medicine and law and the like: a master's and a doctorate. Make sure you know which one is right for you before you start looking for a program.

A master's degree is often more practical in nature than a doctorate. Many teachers, for example, earn master's degrees, and as a result, they are better practitioners in the classroom. They gain an understanding of the philosophy behind certain aspects of teaching, and they work to become as accomplished as possible in the area of classroom performance.

A doctorate, on the other hand, is often much more intellectual in nature, and also more specific. It affords the students the opportunity to delve into the deepest levels of research and study in a specific aspect of the field. While it may not make you a better teacher in the classroom, it will nonetheless offer you the opportunity to truly understand the nature of teaching and of the various educational and philosophical underpinnings of it.

These two degrees also result in different career opportunities, and depending on the field in which you ultimately want to work, one may be better suited than another. A master's in business administration, for example, is all you need in the corporate world, and a doctorate may be considered superfluous. But to work at the highest levels of the field of astrophysics, you may need to possess a doctorate to succeed.

The process of narrowing down your options is not as painful as it may initially seem. All the effort you put into it in the beginning will result in a much easier time in the end.

Now that you know your objectives, you can find out more about particular colleges from various guides that list programs at different schools, such as *Peterson's Guide to Graduate and Professional Study*. These comprehensive directories list programs, as well as areas of expertise and such items as the number of faculty members and who to contact for an application. Peterson's has separate volumes for business, health, education, law, engineering, mathematics, and other areas.

Of course, you should never overlook the Internet as a source of information. Some of the best colleges you will find on the Web allow you to quickly and immediately download their basic application packages.

Here is a method of attack. Use the brochures, calendars, directories, and Web pages to compile a list of potential schools that appeal to you. After you have compiled a list of potential programs, seek advice from as many people you can.

You want to be comfortable wherever you go to graduate school. So it is important to find out what the working and social environments are like at schools that capture your interest.

It is an obvious fact that the more suited your new environment is to you, the more likely your transition to this new life will go smoothly. You will almost certainly want to visit the schools you are interested in, and take a good look at the area around them. Do you need the things associated with a big city, such as culture and major sports? Or do you like small-town life with its friendliness and slower pace?

During your travels, you will almost certainly meet other graduate students. Do you get along with them? Do you seem to connect? You will be making new friends and want to feel comfortable with other students.

Since as a graduate student you will be doing most of your work in libraries and computer centers, you should also check those out. Are they the type of places where you feel comfortable?

There may be some practical considerations outside the strict issue of selecting a school that you will want to consider. For example, if you are married, you might want to consider whether your spouse can find a job near your school. For that matter, if you need to work, is there employment? And what if you have children? Are there facilities for daycare? Is medical insurance possible?

There are also financial considerations. What is the local cost of living? What will your moving costs add up to?

How about another intangible: the quality of life? Do the weather, the cultural life, the people, and the local forms of culture appeal to you? Bottom line: Is this a place where you can have fun?

Other Choices You Will Have to Make

If you are studying at the doctoral level, you typically will be doing your work under the supervision of a faculty member. He or she is responsible for guiding you through the program. In some disciplines, students also study under a particular graduate supervisor at the master's level. There are also variations. Some students in some master's programs complete a year of coursework before being assigned to a graduate supervisor. Another system might involve new graduate students alternating on a rotational basis.

Some programs call for students to be "assigned" to supervisors, while in others, the matchmaking is mostly left up to the student. Often, it is done even before you enroll in the program.

The reason some programs have new graduate students rotate between supervisors is to give students a broader exposure to different viewpoints.

Whatever the system used, the graduate supervisor is an important choice and you want to make the right one. How do you go about it?

If you happen to be applying to a program that asks you to select your supervisor, do some research focusing on individual faculty members. Look for recent publications, such as books or journal articles as well, to see who is doing what.

Many students do not see the benefits of focusing on the prospective supervisor when considering where to apply to graduate school. There are good reasons why it may be better to begin your selection of graduate programs by looking at the individual faculty members and what their research involves. The interests of your supervisor inevitably play an important part in determining your study in graduate school. Not the courses you take, of course, but the nature of your thesis and other research. So you need to know whether a prospective supervisor's interests are compatible with your own.

It is also important to know what your prospective supervisors are interested in so you can write an effective personal statement. You need to have someone you can communicate with and who understands your position.

Finding someone with similar research interests is the easiest part of getting the right graduate supervisor. The best way to do it is to visit the university and interview professors there, if at all possible.

Interpersonal compatibility is desirable because, after all, you do not want to work with someone not to your liking. (Of course, this goes for the supervisor as well). There is only so much you can find out about a person with a short visit, but you should be able to get some idea of compatibility.

Briefly

Noted

"You may get your degree form a university, but you get your education from your advisor."

Anonymous

You might also check the history of students working for a prospective supervisor. How did they fare? Did they finish the program? Did they go on to have productive careers? This should not be hard to determine.

Is your prospective supervisor's research well-funded? Some types of research are expensive and cannot be done on a shoestring budget. Supervisors do not generally accept students with an under-funded budget but it can happen. Students already in a program can give you their informed opinions about whether there are adequate resources or not.

Even if there is funding now, what about in the future? This is another area to concern yourself with. If you feel you do not have the kind of experience to make these judgments, consider finding someone else to help you. You could consult other students — seniors or even graduates —who can help you make your own decision.

Consider also that there are pros and cons in selecting supervisors who are new or more established in their respective fields. Newer supervisors often are able to spend more time with you. On the other hand, the trade-off may be that their funding is less sure. Younger and newer faculty members are often more open and enthusiastic. That happy glow can rub off on you, and it is a pleasing thing to have around. On the other hand, newer faculty members may not yet have an established reputation within their field. Because of that, they may be less able to help you when you need it.

Older and more experienced faculty members will almost certainly have less time for you and your concerns.

They may also have more graduate students to handle. However, their reputations may be more established and their funding more secure.

You need to decide what kind of working relationship you want in a supervisor. Do you need someone looking over your shoulder or do you prefer to work more independently? Talk to prospective supervisors.

Briefly

Noted

A likeable honors student found a graduate program that seemed an excellent match for her interest and talents. The faculty member she found seemed a perfect choice until she found that the supervisor's experiments required intensive computer knowledge. This student was not computer literate. In fact, she was afraid of computers and hesitant to use them for anything but the most elementary uses. The pair split up.

Here are some tips for success in reverse because these are the qualities you may find in terrible advisors:

- In discussing your paper, he or she tells anecdotes about the author to impress on students that the advisor knows much more than the student.

- He or she reads a student paper only one time.

- He or she changes the subject when there are disagreements. For example, say, "We could talk about this forever but I think we are all working on the same basic idea."

- The advisor reacts to a student's suggested readings by saying, "Why in the world are you wasting your time reading that, anyway?"

- The advisor is far more interested in displaying his or her erudition by coming up with catchphrases or buzzwords that have no real meaning.

- The advisor assigns older students to guide younger ones.

- He or she involves students in decision-making for only routine matters such as spending an hour deciding who should be a discussion leader.

- He or she has students handle computer system administration and tell them it counts as research.

- The advisor shares his or her most trivial thoughts with students.

- The advisor avoids any contact with students.

- He or she is never demanding.

- He or she ridicules anyone who asks questions.

- The advisor takes no interest in courses the students are taking.

- He or she mumbles in an apparent attempt to avoid communication with the student.

The quality and success of the research that you do in graduate school depends in large part on your supervisor's providing you with what you need in physical and other resources.

CHAPTER 3

The Practicalities of Applying

How to Evaluate Graduate Programs

Whatever your program, the more information you can gather, the better. Be sure to start early and leave yourself enough time to study catalogs; talk to students, alumni, and professors; and visit schools.

Professional associations are one place to start. Groups such as the American Psychological Association and the American Historical Association have a variety of free or low-cost information on graduate programs. This includes information on program directories, career information, and advice on getting accepted. The information here is focused on specific fields, so you do not have to wade through a lot of extraneous material.

Briefly

Noted

GradProfiles.com is a user-friendly Web site featuring in-depth school profiles. It is sorted by institution name, location, and programs offered.

There are several comprehensive directories in print, on software, on CD-ROM, or online. They list every graduate program, complete with address and phone numbers. If you are still an undergraduate, your career office should be able to provide you with these guides for free. If that is not the case, your local library or bookstore should come in handy.

Of course, you should look at the programs that are of special interest to you, but you should also take into account what is happening in the job market. For example, if you are seeking a doctorate in English, you will want to be aware that jobs at universities are scarce, but there is demand in other areas, such as online book publishing.

You will also want to find out which schools are well-known in your field. There are various groups that publish detailed ratings of graduate schools including *U.S. News & World Report*, which is perhaps the best-known and widely regarded as the most accurate. It is a good idea to order catalogs and applications from schools you have no interest in attending because you will be able to make better comparisons if you know what is out there. Keep in mind, however, that these rankings are subjective. They tell you nothing about the professors, politics, job placement records, or financial-aid possibilities. They are a source of information, but a limited one.

Once you have sorted out a group of programs, it is time for a more detailed examination. The catalog is the obvious place to start, but you should not stop there. Most departments have a chairperson who is also the admissions contact. He or she can put you in touch with current students and alumni who are willing to discuss the various programs. You can also ask questions of the chairperson.

You will want to look at program requirements as well. There are two separate issues to consider: First, most graduate programs generally have suggested undergraduate majors or at least a list of coursework that will provide background for your graduate degree. These requirements or suggestions are listed in the program catalog. Second, each program will have requirements for graduation.

Take a close look at the graduation requirements. Most of these will be filled through coursework, research, or clinical/field work. There is one requirement you want to pay particular attention to, and that is whether or not you need a foreign language. At the master's level, reading ability in another language is sometimes required. At the doctorate level, it is usually required for graduation. We call your attention to this because some students seem to have inherent difficulties in learning another language.

Briefly

Noted

Dave was a brilliant student in college who never went to graduate school because of his own perceived lack of language learning abilities. He was afraid he could not learn another language. When his computer company told him he could not be promoted unless he got a master's degree, he found a school not requiring a foreign language. It was not among the elite schools, but he managed to fulfill the requirement.

Check the opinions of other graduate students. You might be surprised to know that most of them are quite outspoken about the strengths and weaknesses of their professors. Try to contact at least two current students and two recent graduates for a program you are considering. Professional associations also offer you a chance to evaluate people who already have degrees and are working in the marketplace. Some associations sponsor career bulletin boards with new guests each month. These master's degree and Ph.D. holders can answer many of your questions.

The Internet is also a great place to gather information. Bulletin boards, especially on the commercial online services, are good places for exchanging information. There are also online discussion groups and mailing lists specifically for graduate students and prospective students.

Here is something you may have forgotten: the school's location. Why is this important? For one thing, you may remember from undergraduate days, colleges and universities usually give in-state residents a tuition break. The same applies in many grad schools. You will need to check residency requirements since they vary widely. This may involve some planning.

Since you are going to be around for a few years as a graduate student, you will want to approach the subject in the same way someone searches for a new job. What is the quality of life in the school you are thinking of attending? There is also the question of climate. Most of the Ivy League schools and many of the top graduate universities are in the more frigid northern and Midwestern United States. If you are used to a warm climate, you might not find this a welcome change.

Do not forget to look at the faculty, either. You will want to study with the best professors. Ask them questions. Many graduate students apply to a particular department with the thought that a prominent researcher or scholar will be there. This is not always so. You may find the professor you wanted because of his or her fame is unavailable, uncooperative, or simply not interested in working with you. So what do you do then? Someone else will be needed who is perhaps not as desirable.

How much does the faculty work with students? Access to professors is critical, since at the graduate level, most papers and exams are graded by assistants or tutors. At the doctoral level, however, professors are much more accessible. They will generally work with students in small seminar classes and assist in doing research.

Another important issue to consider when it comes to faculty is whether or not the department is stable. Is the faculty nearing retirement age? Say you want to work with a distinguished Ivy League professor. Chances are he or she will have been around for a while. Will he or she be there in five years or so when you finish your doctorate program?

Briefly

Noted

Elizabeth Kies was enrolled in a doctoral program for physics. She wanted to drop a class given by a well-known professor who had published many papers and books in his field. He was going to retire in a year. When she told him she was dropping his class, he became angry (graduate professors have a lot of power and can have huge egos). If she dropped him, the professor said, he would refuse to sit on her committee to graduate. She changed her mind.

You will also want to consider the student body. What are they like? Perspectives that make you liberal in one program can be viewed as conservative in another. Where do you fit with the peers who you will be spending years with?

If you plan on an academic career, your student colleagues will someday be your professional colleagues. You certainly do not want old dislikes surfacing as you are trying to get your first book published or attempting to get tenure.

Catalogs are recommended, but you will not find everything there. For example, the catalog might tell you that 700 assistantships are given each year, but it might not tell you in which departments. Does the school of your choice have several in your own department or perhaps just a handful? This is highly useful information.

Courses are also listed in the catalog, but you will want to know when classes are available. You need to find out in case you have scheduling problems. You will want to know the concentration of courses in your area. Most graduate programs are flexible about part-time studies, but doctoral programs are less so. Many doctoral programs expect a minimum amount of time "in residence," or enrollment as a full-time student. These important issues are often not mentioned in catalogs.

Briefly

Noted

For potential career information, here are three sites:

www.acinet.org *provides salary information for the same job in five or more cities.*

www.jobstar.org *is a site linking to more than 300 salary surveys.*

www.bls.gov *is the Bureau of Labor Statistics Web site, which offers salary data.*

If you are going to graduate school, you have to consider the costs. Finances are always an issue. The most expensive kind of graduate program is generally a terminal master's degree at a private school (which is what you are aiming for). Loans are available, and there are grants and scholarships, but in general, free financial assistance is much harder to find. Most private schools apply the same tuition rate to in-state and out-of-state residents. In a master's program at a top school, you are not likely to find ways to cut tuition costs. Savings will have to come from finding cheaper ways to live and cutting back on housing expenses, among other strategies.

At the doctoral level, you are a little more fortunate because "tuition remission" (free), grants, or stipends are more common. Percentages of doctoral students receiving full "tuition remission" can range from 0 percent to 100 percent. Later chapters in this book will go into more detail on how to put together a financial plan, but this is an issue you should be thinking about.

You need to evaluate the quality of life at schools you are considering. You should also consider various factors such as the weather and the area's cultural offerings. If you are from the sunny south, for example, you might not be deliriously happy in chilly New England. Likewise, if you are from New York City and accustomed to its many cultural offerings, an Ivy League college in a small town might have limited appeal for you.

Do not let the choice of schools intimidate you. You are looking at the top schools, so you cannot go wrong no matter which one you choose.

Meeting Your Personal Interests

If graduate school closely resembles work, and if the degree does not guarantee you the career of your choice, why did one million people enter U.S. graduate programs last year? They did it despite the inherent difficulties.

But what about you? Have you examined your own life and thought about why you are starting this endeavor? Let us take a look at what you might consider to be sure you are fulfilling your own personal interests.

Philosophers encourage you to "know yourself." What does that mean? Knowing yourself is not about "loving yourself" regardless of what you are like. It is also not about berating yourself.

To get to know yourself, you need a certain calmness. You need to be able to see yourself in a detached way without emotion. You need to see yourself as a stranger would see you.

Clearly, we are not wholly unified beings. When you look at yourself, you see many diverse things. You have a social self and a work self. You are angry at times and happy at others. We all contain many parts. When we begin to understand the workings of these parts, we can begin to have a sense of who we are.

Knowing yourself is not abstract naval-gazing. It involves seeing yourself objectively. It means being honest with yourself. It means admitting your faults and not using rationalizations to explain them. You have to realize that knowing the truth about yourself means recognizing your own motivations for what they are.

When someone we respect criticizes us in some way or makes an unflattering observation about us, it is easy to reject that point of view. But when we are objective, we can concede what might be right about what they say.

To know yourself you need to know something about other people as well, because in many ways you are the same as the person down the street. We are all cut from the same cloth. Understanding that idea and knowing a little about psychology can help us learn more about our own motivations and emotions.

The bottom line is that honesty is the best policy. Can you honestly assess your strengths and weaknesses? Careful thought and solid preparation are half the battle. Never be afraid of your negative qualities. Often, moments of failure are more rewarding than moments of success.

Briefly  **Noted**

"Finish each day and be done with it. You have done what you could; some blunders and absurdities have crept in; forget them as soon as you can. Tomorrow is a new day; you shall begin it serenely and with too high a spirit to be encumbered with your old nonsense."

Ralph Waldo Emerson

The primary consideration when trying to decide on your particular course of study is the job you are ultimately seeking. You may already know that to join academia or teach or do research at the university level, you need a doctorate. It is also virtually impossible to work as a clinical or research psychologist without a doctorate. And if you are considering social work, healthcare, or anything in education, the master's degree is the professional qualification you need to move past entry-level jobs.

Here are ten tips gathered from graduate students:

1. Be devoted. It is a long haul.

2. Do not let money be your main motivation.

3. Be sure you know the history of your field. Yes, it may be dull, but it is essential.

4. Sell yourself. You probably do not know how to do it, but you can learn.

5. Read everything you can get your hands on.

6. Learn to think for yourself; do not expect others to do it for you.

7. Thoroughly investigate your preferred school.

8. Get to know professors in the departments of interest to you.

9. Do your studying as quickly as you can; that will help you keep your focus.

10. Know why you are going to school; if you do not know why, your chances of failure are much higher.

Here are some questions to ask for a self-assessment:

- Both in and out of school, what three things do you do best? What three things do you do worst?

- List three experiences that have had the greatest impact on your life. List six activities that you enjoy doing the most.

- Which academic strength has been most useful to you? What are your academic weaknesses? What have you done to overcome these weaknesses?

- List six social strengths that have helped you get along with other people and develop solid relationships. Add one area where you might try to improve.

- How would your parents and your best friend describe you?

- List half a dozen adjectives that describe your strengths and weaknesses.

- What can you contribute to the graduate school you hope to attend? What do you think you will get out of your successful completion of the program? How will it change you?

- Describe your typical day and weekend. What would you change about your schedule?

- Describe a challenge or obstacle you have overcome.

- List what you think are the most important things in life.

Another critical and down-to-earth decision you will have to make is whether you want to attend full-time or part-time. This question is sometimes a no-brainer. Take, for example, a young mother with two children. She will almost certainly opt for part-time studies.

The question of finances is a factor in this decision. If you have to work while pursuing your degree, you will have to consider part-time. Some part-time programs that are ideal for those who cannot go full-time cost more in the long run, but sometimes there is no other choice.

Most part-time students take two to four years to complete their degrees; doctorate programs can take several years. The problem with not going all out is that students sometimes get discouraged or worry about finishing. The drop-out rate is much higher for part-time students than full-time.

Many students in full-time graduate programs support themselves with part-time jobs. If you can do it, the recommendation from most experts is to make an effort to attend school as a regular student. You will graduate quicker and start receiving your financial rewards sooner, and your chances of successfully completing the program are increased.

For a lot of advice at the right price — for free — you should consider your college counselor. He or she should be one of your top sources of information. Consider that the counselors are reasonably impartial and will treat you with fairness. You should be able to count on receiving honest advice from them. What can they do for you? Consider the following as only the tip of the iceberg:

- They can guide and counsel you through the formulation of your school plans.

- They often have an organized resource center with brochures, handbooks, videotapes, and other reference materials.

- They often attend various meetings that inform them about admissions, financial aid, and testing.

- They can coordinate and implement other invaluable information for your needs.

- They might even write letters of recommendation for you.

How to Solve Unexpected Problems such as Missing Paperwork

You breathe a sigh of relief. You have sent out all of your application forms. That is a lot of pages. You are now waiting to hear the results. What do you do if one school or more starts sending you letters telling you that your paperwork is incomplete. Where is the rest of it?

This is impossible, you think. Before you panic, find out

why problems like this come up, and what you can do about them.

Graduate schools get a lot of mail. Often, all these bags of mail come at deadline times. Many schools report that they receive half of their applications just before deadlines. Since some letters of recommendation and other paperwork come from different sources, schools do not always receive all the necessary applications in a single envelope.

Logistically speaking, opening, dating, sorting, and processing applications can be burdensome. Even with armies of workers on hand, the length of the entire operation can take anywhere from four days to three weeks, depending on the size of the school. Quite reasonably, there will be a delay between the arrival of an application at an admissions office and the placement of all information into an individual's file. "Missing" material is often somewhere in the admissions office and has yet to be filed. Letters sometimes are sent to applicants as a sort of insurance.

Other factors also come into play. Letters and packages handled by the U.S. Postal Service are often referred to as "snail mail" for good reason. In our current age of faxes, e-mails, and instant messages, people are used to immediate communication. Sending information through the postal system takes time. When you mail your application, remember that there will be a lag between when you send it and when it is received. Missing information is sometimes en route.

Of course, more and more students are choosing to apply to schools online. With online applications, such as Harvard's, the problems of paper volume and snail mail are seemingly solved, but a new issue emerges. Some applicants do not trust the online application process, so after they send their information electronically, they mail it and sometimes fax it as well. Obviously, this creates double or triple the amount of work for the admissions office staff, and the sorting process takes even longer. So our recommendation is to pick one form of application and stick to it.

How do you know the school has even received your application? That is an easy one. You should receive an acknowledgement by e-mail that your application has been received. If you apply online, you should get this e-mail within a day or two. When it hits your in-box, make sure that all information entered on the application (name, home address, and so on) is correct. Do not hesitate to call the admissions office if you accidentally entered the wrong information or if you do not get the e-mail at all. Every school's guidelines vary, so be sure to review the admissions requirements online before and after you turn in your application to avoid delaying the time it takes for them to consider your application.

How can you check the status of your application, and how often should you check? Most schools have status checks through their admissions office's Web site. The confirmation that tells you they have received your application usually will have a login and password for the school's Web site so only you can see the stage of your application. Receipts of transcripts, letters of recommendation, and test scores are sometimes noted on these status pages, so check back regularly to make sure the required parts of your application have arrived.

Briefly Noted

Layla Matthews, working as a nurse, enrolled in graduate school to teach nursing. But she had been to several colleges. She had to submit transcripts from each college, a time consuming chore. Then, the grad school program where she applied failed to get all her transcripts. So she had to call the colleges again to ask that the transcripts be sent. The moral is that sometimes you have to ask more than once, and you have to stay on top of any such requests.

So what do you do to make sure your application is at least being considered? Here are some steps to take:

1. **Send your applications in a timely manner.** To get college applications in on time, you must send them out several weeks in advance of the school's deadline. This will allow the post office to deliver the material and the staff in the admissions office to process it with time to spare. Even if you are e-mailing your applications, send them in advance just in case any unforeseen issues come up. When you mail your applications in

advance of deadlines, even if material needs to be resent, there is nothing to worry about.

2. **Keep a copy of everything.** Make sure to duplicate your entire application. Also, remember to hang on to notes or e-mails from admissions offices, personal identification numbers and passwords, and even canceled checks. It never hurts to have full documentation of your actions and interactions, especially if a problem crops up later.

3. **Keep your name consistent.** Choose one name and stick with it. If you include your middle name on one document, you must remember to use it on all other forms. If you have a nickname, decide whether you will apply using that name or your given name. Either way, do not switch once you have chosen because the likelihood of mix-ups and missing pieces will undoubtedly increase if you do.

4. **Get the facts.** Even if part of your application is missing, the situation is easily fixed. Avoid angry confrontations with admissions officers or your school counselors. Take a deep breath; find out the problem by calling the college's admissions office; and take the steps necessary, if any, to solve the problem.

So what if you do not hear back from the college where you are applying? Simple common sense tells you that after a reasonable amount of time, you contact the school to ask what happened. It is a good idea to call or contact the school well before deadlines, when the admissions office gets busy.

Another problem frequently encountered by students is getting their letters of recommendation sent out before deadlines. Many people procrastinate when faced with writing a letter. The recommendation here is to give potential references a lot of facts. It is a lot harder to put off writing a letter if someone has a file of material on you and your sterling qualities than if there is a short note. Obviously, you might have to follow up with a brief call or e-mail to ask politely if the letter has been sent.

Sometimes, someone will ask you for a sample letter. It is a good idea to comply and do a great job about it. Some people will simply use your own sample letter. Forget modesty here. Give it your best shot.

Briefly

Noted

It is a good idea to call your potential recommenders a few weeks before the deadline to ask if they have any questions you can answer. It is a low-key way of reminding them they still have not mailed their letters.

How to Conduct Online Research

If you have your own access to the Internet, you can

do your school research from the comfort of your home. Virtually all universities have home pages where potential applicants can access a school's academic calendar and admission information. Sites also let you search for universities by program and provide sources of funding and other valuable information.

The universities you are considering all have Web sites, which you can learn a lot from visiting, although there are large differences in what each program posts. Any department at any university can include whatever it wants to on the Internet. The information is not presented in any standard form. There are also no criteria for what is posted and there is no impartial checking. Always look for a date on the page or some other way to see if the information is still applicable.

Faculty biographies and the academic interests of faculty members are other bits of key information you can find on the Internet. Professors' contact numbers and business offices are also listed, as well as program requirements that include admission standards, areas of emphasis, required courses, and degree options. You can also find what kind of research was done by graduate students, common affiliations with departments on campus, facilities available to graduate students, and links to area attractions.

An informative site will help prospective graduate students identify the programs that match their interests, lead applicants through the college's admission process, notify prospective applicants about assistantships, and list the requirements for the completion of a graduate degree.

It is not recommended that you use only electronic sources to gather information necessary for graduate school. If you combine printed directories with using the Internet, you will have all the information you need for making intelligent decisions.

How do you search the Internet? There are two ways. You can use a directory or a search engine. Among the directories are Yahoo! and Lycos. They will both present you with a set of categories; clicking on one of them leads you to a set of sub-categories. You can continue on this way until you find what you want. The results you get with a directory depend on the topics included, the way they are classified, and the number of sites in the directory.

As you may know all too well, the most frightening part of applying to graduate school for many is taking the GRE. You will almost certainly have to take it as well as other tests. The Internet can help you out in this area as well. There is a lot of information about the tests, as well as sample tests and sales pitches for exam-preparation courses on the Internet. You can also find testing dates and sites, and lists of books to help you prepare. Some students get so panicky about tests, they have difficulty even before the exam starts. By taking a look at the test and practice exams on the Internet, students can at least be prepared for the types of questions they will encounter.

Here are some Internet sites to consider:

- The Association of Medical Colleges, **www. aame.org,** has information on curriculum, school expenses, selection factors, and financial aid information. The site also has admission requirements.

- Chaser, the Resource Center for Graduate Student External Support, **http://chaser.rutgers.edu,** is the Resource Center for Graduate Student External Support at the Graduate School-New Brunswick community. Its major mission is to assist graduate students in identifying and applying for fellowships and research grants to support their graduate work.

- The Chronicle of Higher Education, **www. chronicle.com/news/rss.xml,** has a variety of free news and information that is perhaps of most interest to academics.

- College Board, **www.collegeboard.org,** offers U.S. programs by subject, geographic area, and program level.

- The Council of Graduate Schools, **www.cgsnew. org,** has information for current and prospective graduate students, including publications that can be ordered online. The site also has a section aimed at issues of interest to graduate faculty and administrators. It provides a chance for students to see what educational decision-makers think about current issues.

- Delta Course, **www.deltacourse.com,** offers a free daily GMAT practice question by e-mail. For a fee, the site offers online GMAT study guides and practice questions.

- Emory Colossal List of Career Links, **www. emory.edu/CAREER/Links,** provides job search information as well as access to graduate and professional schools. This site allows searching of schools by program, and provides links to many related sites.

- The Financial Aid Information Page, **www.finaid. org**, contains a comprehensive listing of financial aid resources.

- Get Prepped, **www.getprepped.com,** is a for-profit organization offering weekend, multi-week, and tutoring courses on the LSAT.

- The Graduate Management Admissions Council, **www.gmat.org,** provides a 400-school database along with 200 links to graduate business schools. Students can access GMAT information and register for the test on line.

- Graduate School Guide, **www.schoolguides.com,** has guides to doctoral, master's, and professional degree programs and provides school profiles.

- Kaplan, **www.kaplan.com**, a for-profit organization, offers test preparation exams. The site contains information about their services as well as other topics relating to graduate school.

- The Graduate Student Resource Page, **www-personal.umich.edu,** has a variety of links ranging from advice for getting in, to survival tactics when you are accepted, and even a few humorous references.

- The Law School Admission Council, **www.lsac. org,** provides basic information on schools approved by the American Bar Association.

- MonsterTRAK — ScholarshipTRAK, **www. monstertrak.com,** contains practical information on scholarships.

- The National Association of Graduate-Professional Students, **www.naqps.org,** has a goal of providing support for members, but it also has a lot of valuable information for would-be and graduate students.

- Peterson's Education and Career Centre, **www. petersons.com,** includes information on graduate study, studying abroad, financing your education, distance learning, and more.

- The Princeton Review, **www.princetonreview. com,** is a for-profit organization offering test preparation courses for such grad school exams as the GRE, LSAT, GMAT, and MCAT. The site contains information on their services and general graduate school information including the latest updates on grad school admission tests. The site also offers free online test samples for the GMAT and GRE.

- Project 1000, **http://mati.eas.asu.edu/p1000/whatis.html,** is a national program created to assist under-represented students applying to graduate school. Students may apply to up to seven of the more than eighty-eight participating Project 1000 institutions by using one application. Participation is free to individual students and to the participating institutions.

- The University of British Columbia Career Services, **www.students.ubc.ca/careers/graduate,** is a searchable database of "annotated Web sites rated for relevance to graduate students" compiled by the school. While some of the links are specific to Canada, most are useful to all users. Each listing tells you what you can expect to find at each site: the good and bad points, plus a link to the site. Topics in this list include all facets of the career and job-search process, from self-assessment to making the transition to work.

- U.S. News Online, **www.usnews.com/sections/education/index.html,** provides information on choosing a graduate school, including recent rankings.

- Yahoo!'s Graduate School Directory, **www.wlu. edu/career/yahoo,** includes information on medical, business, and law schools.

Requesting Transcripts and References

Sending in transcripts and references sounds like a simple matter. Unfortunately, this is not a process under your direct control — you have to rely on others. As a result, there is a lot of room for mistakes and confusion. Getting transcripts sent in is no more than clerical work, but it has to be done right.

Every admissions committee wants official transcripts of your grades from all the universities and colleges you have attended, including a school where you took only one course.

Undergraduate GPAs are often heavily weighted by admissions committees. You should know, however, that committees often view a student's grades for the last two years as far more importance than the first two years. Committees also pay attention to the particular courses the student took and performance in a few select courses. If you are taking psychology, for example, committee members would be pleased to see that you had taken some courses in experimental design and statistics. Committee members know these classes will come in handy in psychology since they will be valuable in studying behavioral research.

When weighing your last two years, committees look for trends. A rising record with better grades often leads the committee to see your candidacy is coming into its own — that you are maturing and improving yourself. You will want to be able to show your grades are getting better; if not, you are what is known as a "sliding student. You may have your reasons, but you have to find other factors that compensate for this deficiency.

Consider that admissions offices would much rather see steady improvement from a candidate than steady performances or a marked downward trend.

Briefly  **Noted** *It is a good idea not to slacken in your senior year. Stay focused. A subpar semester can be devastating to your chances of being accepted.*

To avoid delays when asking schools to send transcripts, telephone the institution first to find out the cost. Mail a check to cover the cost along with your request. Allow plenty of time for your records to be sent. You may need to ask more than once for the records to be sent. That is a good and useful follow-up policy.

Most programs will send you a card or letter saying either that they have received all of the required material or that something was missing. The missing pieces are most likely to be transcripts or letters of recommendation.

Universities are inundated with paper, so be sure to stay on top of this process.

Some students who are not entirely sure where they want to go sometimes want to submit applications to different programs at the same university. Whether or not you can do that depends on the school. Some schools forbid applying to more than one degree program within the university; other schools permit it. You will need to find out the school's policy on this matter.

References are very important — all programs require them. An enthusiastic letter can give you a tremendous boost. Usually, at least some recommendations must be from faculty members. The committee wants to know how good a student you will be and assumes that the best answer will come from those who know you professionally. Obviously, it is best if you can provide some recommendations from people who have a connection with your field. If you are applying to be a youth counselor, for example, a letter from someone in an advanced computer science program probably is not going to be taken seriously. Letters from friends and neighbors are also not useful. Recommendations from those who know your academic abilities are highly regarded.

There are a lot of myths about recommendations, such as the importance of getting a well-known personality or your father's influential friend to boost your chances. Wrong. This could even backfire because any recommendation from a writer who does not know you well can work against you. Another myth is that you want recommendations from a teacher who gave you straight As. Wrong, again. Let us say you got those As in easy courses. This will not improve your chances. Admission committees are generally familiar with "easy" classes and give lower marks to them.

Another common misconception among students is that writing recommendations is part of a teacher's job. So they will do it well, no matter what, right? Teachers are not obligated to write letters, so a little prompting and care on your part is the best approach here. Do not expect your teachers to help you in this area, but ask them politely and chances are they will be glad to cooperate with you.

How do you get good letters? There are several criteria. For example, the person you are asking to send a letter should know you well. He or she should be able to cite specifics rather than generalities such as "Tom is a good student and a fine fellow." That kind of clichéd observation is meaningless. If the recommender can cite some of your specific accomplishments such as winning a coveted prize at a science show, your letter will have much more appeal.

One thing you should do is provide your would-be supporters with a list of your accomplishments. Even if they already know you and what you have done, it is helpful to remind them. Do not assume your proposed recommender is going to recall your every accomplishment.

You can ask for "open" recommendations written for you, which means that you can read the letter provided it is on file in your department or in the placement office. This is not a good idea, since letters are usually accompanied by a form that indicates if the letter is open or not. Admission committee members know that the person writing the reference was aware the student could read it and that there is a better chance that the letter-writers will not be honest under these conditions. Rather than undercutting your own credibility, it is a better practice to let the recommendations remain closed.

If you are unsure what someone is going to say about you, you should simply skip him or her and go on to someone else. This is not an area where you want to take any chances.

Do not send in a name as a reference without telling the person. If someone unexpectedly receives a form with your name on it, and a space for a recommendation, you cannot be sure what the reaction will be, but it almost certainly will not be positive. There have been cases where the proposed recommender simply threw out the request, perhaps thinking it was an advertisement.

Hopefully, you have prepared your teachers for your request. You have spoken up in class and shown a sense of active participation. You have always been prompt. You did all your required assignments, on time, and you even asked to do extra work. You were polite, friendly, and helpful to your teacher and your classmates. Hopefully, if you have had any problems in class, you went to the professor's office to discuss it with him or her. You have shown an interest in how you are doing. That is obviously important. Grades are important as well, but so is the human contact. It is also helpful if you have asked informed questions in class to demonstrate not only your interest but your desire to perform well.

Ideally, when you ask for a recommendation, the professor will already know and perhaps even have talked about possible graduate schools with you. If you have done your job well, your teacher might even volunteer to write a recommendation.

Start this process by contacting faculty members who taught courses in which you did well. Be sure to begin this process at least two months before the deadline for application materials. You should also complete this early enough in the term so professors and others are not racing to grade tests and term papers before the semester ends. If they put it off, as often happens, you may find yourself not even being considered because your basic paperwork was missing.

There is a preferred way of approaching your professors to ask for a recommendation. It is not a good idea to simply walk into a professor's office and ask bluntly for a recommendation. Instead, when you contact him or her, provide a resumé with some of your accomplishments. You might want to mention where the course took you and what you learned. If the professor or recommender does not remember much about you, your resumé will help him or her recall.

Briefly

Noted

A good way to approach professors to ask for a recommendation is to say, "I am applying to graduate school at Harvard. Do you feel comfortable in writing me a good letter of reference?"

You should be able to tell whether a teacher is going to write you a good recommendation by what they say when asked. If they seem to agree halfheartedly, consider going elsewhere. You may have to rely on instincts here, but err on the side of caution. If the professor says no, you should take it politely and move on to others.

You would never ask a professor who clearly dislikes you for a letter of recommendation. By the same token, you might want to consider the professor's own style. Can they write good letters? Can you be the judge of that? Sure, you can see indications in their responses to your own papers. Admission committees love stories and good quotes. Has your professor given you any indication that they could or would provide that? You should offer a little help by giving your professor your resumé and a list of your qualifications, and why you think you would do well in graduate school.

Different programs require different numbers of recommendations. It is good advice to submit perhaps one or more letters than the minimum if at all possible, but do stick to the admission office standards. There is no point in having a dozen letters written if the school only wants two. Admissions committees are busy enough without having to read a lot more paperwork, and they might even hold it against you.

CASE STUDY: J. SCOTT KEOGH

J. Scott Keogh, an associate professor in Evolutionary Biology at the Graduate Program in Ecology, Evolution, and Systematics at the Australian National University, has advised and written many recommendation letters for students. Here, he explains the wrong and right way to approach a potential advisor (or someone for a letter of recommendation) by e-mail:

Things have changed in the last few years regarding how students make first contact with a potential advisor. Almost always this now happens via an informal e-mail rather than a formal letter or a phone call. What few students realize is that advisors get these e-mails all the time and the more famous the advisor and the more prestigious the university, the more this happens. It would not be unusual for some potential advisors to be approached by 50 or more potential Ph.D. students in a year.

What this means is that the initial approach is very important because you must differentiate yourself from the other 50, but many students get opportunities quickly shut down simply because their initial approach is inappropriate. The mistake most students make is to not provide the critical information that a potential advisor actually wants to know. By far

CASE HISTORY: J. SCOTT KEOGH

the most common e-mail I get as both a potential advisor and also in my capacity at a large graduate program is a very short message stating that they are interested in a particular area, are looking for an advisor, and then ask about funding opportunities. What's wrong with that? The problem is that there is no information content in the e-mail that would actually pique the advisor's interest in taking on that student. Upon receiving this e-mail, some advisors will start a dialog and ask for more information, some will never respond, and many will write back saying something along the lines of 'I'm very sorry, but I'm not taking on any new students at the moment.'

If you think about it from an advisor's point of view, what is the critical information they want to make a judgment on a potential student? They want to know your grades, your experience in the field, if you have won any awards, your motivation and aspirations, why you want to do a research degree, and why you want to come to their lab. Advisors are human and react the same way as other people react. The Ph.D. process and the student-advisor relationship is long and complex. Because an advisor knows this and a potential student often does not, potential advisors respond best to potential students who have made a clear case for why they have been chosen.

The initial approach should be a well-thought-out letter that has been specifically written for that advisor and does not sound like a form letter that you are sending out everywhere (even if you are). Form letters get deleted. The e-mail should contain information about the following areas, approximately a paragraph each:

1. Demonstration that you are familiar with the advisor's research.

2. Explanation of your research interests and also your aspirations (for example, why you want a Ph.D.).

3. Explanation of how your interests mesh in with the research already happening in the advisor's group.

4. Explanation of your academic grades and test scores if you have them, regardless of what they are like (you cannot hide them for long). If your grades are poor but your GRE scores are good, point that out. If your grades are good and your GRE scores low, point that out. If your grades and GRE scores are both low, you will need to put even more effort into points 1, 2, and 3.

5. Explanation of any research experience you already have. Be honest if you do not have any and put even more effort in to points 1, 2, 3, and 4.

6. Attach a detailed résumé or Curriculum Vita (CV).

If you provide that level of information, the potential advisor is virtually obligated to make an effort to help you. After a chat has been started and if the recommender seems interested, you could go for a visit. If that has not convinced him or her, however, take our earlier advice to move on to another person.

If you graduated a few years ago, it might be more difficult to get recommendations from your former professors. So what do you do in that case? Most professors keep their grade books and can see what grade you earned a few years back. That gives the professor some idea of how you did. But if he or she does not remember much about you, it is your job to supply up-to-date information on your courses under the professor and what you have been doing since then. If the approach is by letter, you can supply all the necessary information in writing, including in your cover letter that you will call to discuss further the possibility of a recommendation. Assuming you have a resumé, you should also send that on to your professor. If you do not have a resumé, you should get one.

Keep in mind that your best recommendation is a strong letter from a faculty member at the school where you are applying. If this is possible, it will certainly help you in being accepted. One reason for this is that admissions committee members will hesitate to override the judgment of a colleague who has had personal contact with an applicant. It is also a bit awkward to tell coworkers that his or her candidate did not make the cut. That is almost like a personal repudiation or a "slap in the face." Professors are humans, too, with human feelings.

The Personal Interview: How to "Ace" It

Let us be candid about it: The prospect of an interview can be little less than terrifying. You sit in an office and see the last interviewee stagger out. His hair is ruffled and his clothing is wrinkled. He looks like he has been sweating. Your name is called. You exchange glances with other faces in the waiting room and walk through the door. Your collar feels tight. Your legs feel like strands of spaghetti. You are *scared.*

It does not have to be this way, of course. By this stage of your application, you should have some confidence. You have thought about your strengths and weaknesses. You have thought about the questions that will be asked. If you take that one extra step and familiarize yourself with the interviewing strategies found here, you should be able to walk into that interview room with a spring in your step. You are not afraid at all. You are eager, in fact, to get on with this personal interview because you are prepared, and you know you will perform persuasively.

The interview can be particularly troubling to shy and retiring people and to those who dislike talking about themselves. It is not uncommon for individuals who present strong cases on paper for acceptance to do poorly in the interview phase because they do not have an engaging personality lack the confidence to communicate well. This can be unfortunate, but if you consider yourself among that group, you can increase your chances of doing well by solid preparation. If you are in that group, you might also want to start practicing your communication skills. Read some books on the subject. Practice the suggestions you find in your reading. All your life, you will be going through interviews, whether they involve education or your occupation. You will be judged on how well you perform. It is clearly worth making an effort to acquire a skill that you will need throughout your life.

The first thing to do to prepare for your upcoming interview is to look through all your notes written during the application process. This will remind you of the type of accomplishments you will want to cite during your interview. Take a careful look at the positive areas of your life. Do not skimp on this part of your preparation. Interviewers invariably cite inadequate preparations as the major reason students do not do well during a personal meeting.

An interview is a two-way street. You will also want to ask the interviewer questions. Why is this important and what kinds of questions should you be asking? By asking questions, you reinforce your interest in the school's program. Your interest in the school is an important part of your interviewer's evaluation. Of course, you should choose questions that illustrate your knowledge of the program. A broad question that shows you have not done your homework may harm your candidacy. Another reason to ask questions is to demonstrate your conversational skills and confidence. There is still another reason for your own benefit — to help you find out more about the school.

You do not want to take control of the conversation with your questions, but you should display an interest in the interviewer. This is not the type of frivolous conversation you might have with a friend, such as discussing how the New York Yankees did against the Boston Red Sox. But there are legitimate areas of interest of a personal nature such as what the interviewer thinks of the college, for example, and how he or she came to his or her present position. Remember that an interview is also a dialogue. It is a conversation. It is a chance to let you find out more about the school from somebody who works there or who went there.

It is always a good idea to subtly get around to your own accomplishments. You may be asked to describe your work experience outside of school, for example. If you can make this relevant to the work involved in your field, you get extra points. Do not assume the interviewer has carefully read your personal statement and does not need to hear it, either.

At some point, you should try to prepare for any questions that may be asked. You cannot be sure what will come up, of course, but there are some typical questions that appear often. Your planning may involve questions that will not come up, but you should be prepared and you should practice your answers to tough questions. The following are some questions and hints on how you might want to answer them:

- **How do you know about their program?** Your answer might cite others who have benefited and been successful after completing the program.

- **Why do you think it is the right program for you?** Here, tailor your answer to be in sync with the program. Perhaps it covers many of your personal interest areas, for example.

- **What aroused your interest in the program?** Here, you can repeat a little history of your own progression and how you came to apply to this particular program.

- **Where do you see yourself in 10 or 20 years?** You can relate this question to the program by explaining what it is you want to be doing in your chosen field, whether it is being a psychology teacher or a scientific researcher working on a cure for cancer.

- **What are your weaknesses?** This question comes up repeatedly. Do not be flippant and say you have trouble responding to your morning alarm clock. Turn this question around. Perhaps you speak first and think later. You will probably want to mention some negatives because, after all, everyone has them no matter how near perfection they are. But whatever you answer, you can point out how you are trying to improve some defect. Be as specific as you can. If you say you sometimes procrastinate, for example, recall a recent incident where you finished work well before a deadline.

- **Tell us about yourself.** This is a common request. It may be difficult for you to respond to because it is so general and broad in scope. After all, where do you begin? This question can be turned to your advantage simply because it allows you to make any answer you wish. To prepare for this question, write down your skills before the interview. Be prepared to speak for two minutes about your outstanding skills. Do not demean yourself or say something such as "I'm nothing special." You are special. You only need to explain why.

- **What are your career goals?** This is a fairly easy question if you have thought about it. You want to show that you have definite plans and specific goals. If you say something such as that you want personal growth or to achieve your maximum potential, the interviewer will see that answer as too vague. Frame your answer in a way that fits into the type of training and education you expect from graduate school.

- **Are you the right candidate for our program? Why?** These are recurring questions that can be expressed in many different ways. If you have done your homework, you should know enough about the program to discuss specific aspects.

The goal is to merge your own qualifications with the goals of the program.

Interviewers want to know that you are sincerely interested in their programs. You can show your own interest by citing specific strengths of the program, or you might point out that you know they have good people and that you know your training will be top-notch.

More questions might involve your strong points. You might respond that focus and commitment are always good qualities. You do not need a lot of answers here, but you should be able to pinpoint two or three of your most admirable traits.

You will almost certainly not remember all the tips and suggestions you have read. So why not enlist a friend to help you practice? If you are on good terms with a professor, you might consider asking him or her to help you. If you do not have the time or anyone handy to perform this role, try an imaginary interview by yourself. Ask questions and listen to your answers.

How long should your interview last? Generally, the better interviews are 30 to 45 minutes. If your interview lasts for an hour or more, you know the interviewer is interested in your candidacy.

Remember to be relaxed. You are not hanging out with your friends, but this is not a visit to the White House either.

Dress as if you were going to school or perhaps a little more formal. Be natural. Basically, you want to be clean and presentable. Some other do's:

- Do arrive early. If you have time or are staying overnight, you will want to check exactly where the interview is taking place, and how long it will take to get there. Do a dry run beforehand, if possible.

- Do shake hands firmly when you enter the room. Look your interviewer in the eye during your talk. Speak in complete sentences.

- Do get the interviewer to talk about him- or herself. That not only shows maturity, but everyone likes to talk about themselves. So you will be earning points from the interviewer for many reasons.

- Do talk about yourself. The interviewer is there to weigh your candidacy and he or she will need to hear all there is to know from you.

And some do not's:

- Do not be shy or retiring in any way.

- Do not fidget.

- Do not bite your nails.

- If you think you know more than the interviewer, do not show off.

- Do not try to come across as perfect or flawless. Psychological studies have proven time and again that people with a few flaws or imperfections are much better liked than people who appear to be without any hang-ups.

- Do not make the mistake of thinking that the interviewer wants to hear only about your good qualities.

Consider just what the interviewer is looking for. He or she wants to know about your interpersonal skills, for example. The interviewer also wants to make a determination on whether you can handle the challenges and demands of a highly selective institution. He or she wants to know your overall potential. Motivation is another consideration. The interviewer wants to see that you are serious about your goals and ambitions. He or she wants to determine areas you are passionate about. Overall, the interviewer will be determining your most impressive qualities as well as the flaws that might make you unsuccessful.

Be sure to have four or five questions of your own at the end of your interview. Your choice of questions should be made as your interview proceeds. There is a good chance you have not absorbed every subject covered in your exchange, so be sure to ask questions about areas you do not understand. If you want to be bold, at the end, ask the interviewer whether or not he or she thinks you are a good match for the school. Hopefully, you will get an honest answer that will help you plan your next move. If the interviewer turns around and asks you whether you would go to the school if accepted, you are under no obligation to answer unless you are positive this is the right school for you.

A highly professional way to end the interview is with a handshake. Ask for a business card and e-mail address. It is good manners (and politically correct as well) to write a note thanking the interviewer. You will also earn points by raising a few questions, illustrating your interest and, hopefully, your intelligence.

How to Overcome Lower Grades

Your chances of getting into a top graduate school are better if you have a high GPA. That is a fact, though you may not like it. Many studies found that overall, students with excellent grades as undergraduates did better in graduate school. Critics of these studies point out that they involved general groups, and perhaps did not take individuality into account. So let us say you had a less-than-stellar GPA. By now, you have read that this does not mean the end of the world, or that you cannot get accepted at graduate school.

The other side of this issue is that students with excellent GPAs and the highest grades in their graduating class cannot be overconfident or complacent about being accepted. Many of these top students fail to get into the top graduate schools because they have no idea what they are doing when they apply. They do not understand what the graduate committees are looking for in applicants. These sometimes-arrogant students can unwittingly sabotage themselves by not dealing properly with all aspects of the admission process or by taking it for granted that their past work will surely get them accepted.

Before you get too worried, consider the following questions about your grades: Did you get most of the Cs in your freshman and sophomore years? Have your grades improved as a junior and senior? Perhaps your GPA overall would improve dramatically if you excluded your grades in the first two years. Consider that many programs place more emphasis on the grades from the most recent undergraduate years. There is hope in that fact.

In some disciplines, there are some undergraduate courses that are particularly important for graduate school. Some programs look closely to see whether you have taken those courses and the grades you obtained there. These grades may be more heavily weighted than grades in other courses. Your strategy, in that case, would be to calculate your GPA without that first year or two during which you had low grades; and calculate what your GPA is in the courses most relevant to your academic interest. If that helps, you can indicate this in your cover letter or in your essay.

If you are in your senior year, of course, there are not a lot of chances to improve your grades, but you can do an unclassified year of undergraduate work to improve your GPA. You can also take some of the special courses preferred by graduate programs in your field. Some schools do not consider applicants unconditionally, but invite them to enroll in select undergraduate courses for one or more semesters with the thought of granting formal acceptance when you prove you can do the necessary work.

If you have lower grades, the trick is to provide a lot of evidence that your GPA does not accurately reflect your abilities and ambitions. In other words, the GPA is not indicative of your real potential. Some programs will let you put more emphasis on work experience. You might be able to overcome a relatively weak overall GPA by undertaking a demanding independent study or research project that demonstrates your true abilities and possibly generates strong letters of recommendation.

Some schools will list a minimum GPA, but that figure reflects the minimum as opposed to the typical threshold figure or average GPA of those admitted. Schools are often reluctant to list average GPA and GRE information because they are only part of the package examined in the decision-making process. You may be able to get more concrete information by contacting a department or program and asking, "In the past few years, what kind of grades and scores have your typical students had to be accepted?"

Briefly

A key to your success is to do things that set you apart from other applicants. Always keep that in mind.

Noted

Another way to offset your low GPA is to excel when you take the GRE. This can be convincing if you score high in areas of real importance to your school. The best advice is to get a sample GRE test and take it with the mindset that it is the real thing. Do it in silence, without breaks. If your score is a critical factor in admission it is a good idea to take a test prep class.

Check to see if your school of interest has an absolute cutoff GPA that is required for application. If you do not meet this absolute cutoff and have extenuating circumstances such as illness, a family crisis, or even poor performance in an unrelated area, ask an admissions officer to find out if exceptions are allowed. If you are eligible to apply but are below the average GPA accepted, most applications include a space where you can address other concerns. This provides a chance for you to mention any extenuating circumstances. Keep these explanations to a minimum.

There are also other ways to offset poor grades. For example, on your application and personal statement, you can accentuate your strengths, such as work experience or leadership positions.

Briefly

Noted

"Let me tell you what has led me to my goal. My strength lies in my tenacity."

Louis Pasteur

One problem with GPAs is the grade inflation that has characterized recent years in public schools. In many cases, admissions officers are aware of grade inflation at certain schools. In addition, there is the issue of what an A grade means at a school in Birmingham, Alabama, versus a school in Beverly Hills, California. As a result, admissions officials have to weigh other data such as class rank and standardized test scores.

Even if your grades were not that good, your class ranking may be an offsetting factor. Class ranking is valuable because it provides some level of student comparison, admissions officials generally say. They are often less concerned with absolute class rank than they are in detailed and helpful tools to determine the top scholars within any given school. Absolute rank has become somewhat less important in the last few years because ranking policies at many schools have changed. Also, many schools have moved away from any type of ranking because of parent pressure. Parents often argue that class rank does not accurately portray the performance of their children.

CASE STUDY: DAVID E. IRWIN Ph.D.

Some good advice for graduate students: Spend at least some time volunteering— perhaps during summer break or on an afternoon off. You might work in a research lab or spend an afternoon at a local hospital's behavioral health center, suggests David E. Irwin, Ph.D., University of Illinois. He says the best applicants often show how they have gained real-world experience by working at a summer camp for children with autism or for a suicide hotline. It shows commitment to the field and, at the same time, provides you with a good idea of what you are getting into.

Another factor to consider is whether or not you were an honors graduate. The term "honors" has several different meanings in undergraduate programs. One meaning is its most common usage, which recognizes that a student has an outstanding GPA. Even though the term "honors student" may be listed as a program requirement, it does not follow that you cannot get accepted without such a designation. Admissions officers know that honors programs do not always reflect true accomplishments. Once students are accepted into such a program, their grades often improve because of the perception they are the best students. Admissions officers are aware of this perception and sometimes ignore or give less weight to the designation "honors" student. Experienced admissions officers also work hard at getting to know the various schools. They read the school profiles, compare course loads between students, and often call high school counselors to ask about classes and grades. A factor they consider that might work to your advantage is that they are aware of the most demanding curriculums. A student who took difficult courses and scored slightly lower than someone who took easy classes may end up the winner, despite lower GPAs.

At the same time, there is flexibility in the definition of what makes up a challenging curriculum. Admissions officers often do not penalize students who attend small or poor schools with limited college preparatory classes because there was no opportunity to take advanced classes.

If you are an honors student, you do have some advantages, because the aim of many honors programs is to prepare students for graduate school. Much of what students do as undergraduates is similar to what they will be required to do as graduate students. For example, many honors programs require students to do an independent research paper. This paper can resemble a master's thesis in many respects, though it does not have the same standards of evaluation. Preparing such a paper is an excellent introduction to what you will have to do in graduate school.

So do not get dejected by lower grades. Most programs will take a close look at your GPA, but you improve your chances of overcoming that by getting into a department program where the research orientation is similar to yours. Your academic record is also far from the only criteria for acceptance. Admissions officials also look at your relevant volunteer, internship, or work experience; how well you do during your personal interview; letters of recommendation; your essay and other written materials; and your score on various standardized tests.

Rejected? So What Do You Do Now?

Shriek! Sob! Woe is me! Despite all your careful preparation, you were turned down. First, do not panic. There are remedies. View this not as a dead end, but a detour. Like many other things in life, it can be overcome and might even act as an incentive to help you improve your second chance to be accepted.

Remember also that, statistically speaking, you have a lot of company. Many doctoral programs receive 10 to 50 times as many graduate applicants than they can take. As many as 75 percent of graduate applicants invited for interviews are not accepted to graduate schools.

That may not make you feel any better, but knowing more about the process may help you decide what to do next. For example, do you know why so many applicants are rejected? The simple answer is that there are not enough places. All graduate programs — whether they involve the top schools or an average institution — receive far more qualified candidates than they can accept. But you are more interested in yourself, of course, so first, you must figure out why they may have rejected you.

In all honesty, there is no real way to tell for sure. In

many cases, applicants are rejected — even if they are seemingly qualified — because they are a poor fit. That means that their interests and career aspirations do not fit the requirements of a particular program.

You might be able to ask the graduate advisor why you were turned down. Write a polite letter or call him or her. You might get an idea why you were turned down, but it is far more likely that you will receive a polite rejoinder that tells you little. So what? You have tried. You will have to find other, less direct ways to find out the reasons for your rejection.

Hopefully you are not too discouraged. As you take on the job of playing detective to find out why you were rejected, look for support from family, friends, and professors. This is a time in your life when it is important to seek social support. Acknowledge that this was a disappointment. Feel free to be upset and acknowledge your feelings, but then move forward. Reassess your own goals. Ask some hard questions and try to answer them honestly. For example: Did you give enough time and attention to all elements of your application, even areas you did not particularly enjoy, such as your essay (a lot of students do not find writing at the top of their list of favorites) or your resumé, or other elements of your application that perhaps did not thrill you?

Your answers to these questions may help you determine whether to reapply next year, apply to another master's program instead, or choose another career path. If you are firmly committed to attending graduate school, consider reapplying next year.

It is possible that your rejection might not have had anything to do with you or your application program. The professors reviewing your application could have had different interests than yours, or they could have simply made a mistake and turned away applicants who would have done well in their program.

Let us take a brief detour and theorize that you are accepted, but on a waiting list. What should you do?

The best advice is to write a letter explaining how you were disappointed that you were placed on the waiting list, but that the school is still your top choice and you are almost positive you would accept an invitation to attend.

Cite a few reasons why the department is a good match for you, even if you already mentioned those in your personal statement. At this point, do not mention any specific professors or research groups because those groups may have already accepted as many students as they want or can afford.

Other new elements you can introduce include new grades; any courses now underway, especially if they are at the graduate level; future plans if they are related to the school; descriptions of any new awards or honors; and revised letters of recommendation.

It is a good idea to continue corresponding with the department to show genuine interest as well.

CASE STUDY: CALEB JOHN CLARK

Graduate degree holder Caleb John Clark found acceptance at three graduate schools before earning his master's from San Diego State University. Below, from his Internet site, are some of the failures he overcame:

- UC Berkeley, 2004/2005.

God I love this school! I tried twice in the Journalism Masters, visited, and flirted with the SIMSs school. Great school. Heavy competition. Didn't click. Didn't get in.

- Claremont Graduate School and University of San Diego, late 1990s/2003.

I messed around with applying to a Ph.D. program here, but it was always panicky and during times when I was depressed. My former professors were patient, but I never got it together to fully apply. Looking back, I was just flailing around and trying to get back to the safety of graduate school near where I went for my masters.

- Harvard. Ed.D. in Educational Technology, 2004.

My boss at the time was an alumnus. He let me write a recommendation that he edited and sent it. I didn't visit. It was more of a halfhearted stab in the dark.

- MIT Media Lab, 2003

Visited. It was a very engineering/programming-focused place and it felt like a fortress in terms of getting in. It was a fantastic place, but I didn't have the chops or what they were looking for, and I didn't click with a professor.

CASE STUDY: CALEB JOHN CLARK

- Stanford Educational Technology Ph.D., Carnegie Mellon University Human-Computer Interaction, 2001.

Visited. They were taking only five new students . . . from the entire world! Oy! It went well, but I felt a little under-qualified. CMU and Stanford were hard to get into and my low GREs and math skills were not helpful, to say the least.

To help in deciding what to do if there is no waiting list but a simple rejection, let us take another look at the actual admission decision — theirs as well as yours.

The start of the application process differs from one school to another. Some schools give the authority to the graduate school itself in the central administration; in other schools the authority is given to individual departments. Either way, faculty is involved in evaluating your application.

A group often does an initial review of the applications, making a first attempt at separating possible acceptances from clear rejections. Common mistakes that disqualify applicants early include incomplete paperwork or someone who displays a serious lack of preparation.

The next phase is when committee members review applications in more detail. Each group settles on favorite candidates. These are presented to the group and the committee makes its final choices. During the later stages, the selection process gets more detailed. In the final stage of the proceedings, your contacts with the department — professors you have spoken with, a visit or an interview — weighs heavily in your favor. If you have impressed a professor and he or she wants to work with you, you will have an advocate. This is a time when your personal statement is important. If there are weaknesses in your application, the personal statement can help tip the balance in your favor.

So You Missed Out Somewhere

Here are some things you can do next time to give you an edge, albeit often only a small one:

1. Apply earlier. Avoid the last six weeks before the deadline.

2. Visit the school again and talk to faculty members you would like to work with. Read some of their recently published work beforehand.

3. Go to summer school in your subject and do well. It is easier to get into summer school just about anywhere.

4. Get volunteer or internship experiences in your subject and do well (even part-time or unpaid).

5. Consider working in a real job in your field. There is no substitute for actual work experience. Get recommendations from supervisors in the field.

6. Get older and try again — sometimes, that is all it takes.

So What You Can Do Now, in More Detail

Try Again

Applying to graduate school is much easier when you are already familiar with the process. Most people's test scores improve when taking the tests again because they know the format and challenges and therefore know how to prepare properly. Similarly, if you have already written application essays, you are familiar with the basic procedure and can hone your skills with your new essay. You can also have your essays edited by someone who can help you make them the best possible.

Improving Your Application

Carefully review everything in your application. Look for ways to improve all the documentation you have prepared. Also, reassess your personal interview. Did you ace it? When you are reapplying to the same school that turned you down, you have a built-in problem: You will have to change committee members' minds. They will have your previous year's application, so you will have to come up with dramatic differences in your latest try at getting in. This can be done if you take a careful look at your options.

Look at Your References

Another key factor to the application process is references. Improving references can be tricky since it does not depend solely on you. If you did not take advantage of providing professors with a clear resumé and helpful information, doing so can improve the recommendations they provide. You can also look for different people to provide you with recommendations.

Take More Tests

You cannot change your undergraduate grades, which may have been a major factor in being turned down, but you can improve two important parts of your application: test scores and your essay. You can take the GRE or the test for your professional field again. You will almost certainly do better because you know the format and should be able to prepare more thoroughly. Many but far from all programs will look at your most recent tests scores and discount earlier ones.

Take the necessary time to prepare for a new test. Let us say you can show a dramatic difference in your more recent effort. Admissions people will take that into consideration.

Improving Your Essay

As for your essay, many graduate students say this is the hardest part of their applications. Students do not know what the faculty wants and worry about what they should say. Since it is difficult to judge what you have written because you are so close to it, do something you might not have the first time – try to get someone knowledgeable in the field to criticize your first effort.

Trying Elsewhere

Since you are looking at the top schools, you are under the disadvantage of having a limited amount of colleges. But perhaps during your research you encountered other universities that also had programs of interest. You have learned a lot about your options. So choose a place that you find acceptable and try next year.

Different Application

If you had originally applied to a school as a doctoral candidate and were not accepted, you may want to look into a master's degree program as a jumping off point. The requirements are generally less stringent. After completing a master's you will have demonstrated your commitment to graduate study and should have a far easier time being accepted to the doctoral program of your choice.

Try Nondegree Student Programs

Another similar option is to apply as a nondegree student. This will generally enable you to take classes with the other degree candidates, allowing both you and your professors to see if you can handle the work. Students who choose this path often have the opportunity to make an extremely positive impression on the professors guiding the acceptance process and when their application comes up the following year, they can have references included from the department to which they are applying.

How to Evaluate School Offers

Here is the other side of the coin: the school or schools made you an offer. But just because they have chosen you does not mean you have to choose them, does it? Of course not.

In all likelihood, you will want to attend the school that has chosen you. After all, you chose them first. But you might want to consider a few other factors before finally committing.

If you have been accepted at two or three top schools, you will want to make comparisons. But first, how does the process work? The letter comes. You have been accepted. Most programs have a standard date, April 15, by which time you must notify the department of your acceptance for the fall semester. Generally, schools hold these openings until that date. If you do not send in your acceptance by then, the offer will be withdrawn.

Generally, if you are accepted at multiple schools, there is a flurry of telephone calls at the last minute as schools make adjustments to the number of students or other factors come up, such as students changing their minds. Because of that, you probably do not want to commit too early. You can fax your acceptance at the last minute.

When you are absolutely sure you want to accept an admission offer, call or e-mail your contact for the program and follow up with a written letter that is faxed and then mailed to the program. A short, professional-looking note indicating that you have made your decision and are pleased to accept their offer of admission is adequate. Tailor the letter to your own style and needs. Be sure to sign the letter above your typed name.

This letter does not have to say much. Here is an example:

> Dear Dr. Smith (or Admissions Committee):
>
> I accept your offer to enroll in the business program at Harvard University. Thank you for your time and consideration, which was greatly appreciated. I am looking forward to attending your program this fall and am excited by the opportunities that await me.
>
> Sincerely,
>
>
> Rebecca R. Student

Briefly Noted

A famous Ivy League medical school had 30 too many acceptances one year; the next year, for one reason or another, they had 30 too little. There were a lot of last-minute telephone calls.

If you are fortunate enough not to have to worry about

money, your choices are simpler. But if you will need financial help, your most important consideration is money. You will want to check out the amount of funding you are being offered. Is it enough for the next couple of years? Will you need to look for financial sources outside of the school? The basic issue is take-home pay after tuition and taxes have been paid. Your housing is one of the most expensive items you will be facing. How much will housing cost at your college? You may want to consider whether the school provides medical insurance, particularly if you have children. Everyone knows how expensive medical insurance is if you have to pay for it yourself. This is a practical consideration you should not ignore.

How about your expected workload? There is a good chance you will teach class or work in a research laboratory. How many hours are expected of you? The prevalent work load is about 20 hours per week averaged over a semester. But if you are doing research, the workload can be much heavier. Another question is whether or not you have been offered a teaching or research assistantship.

Assuming you have visited the school once before, you will want to take a return trip. At this time, after doing your research, you should have a better idea of the school's general atmosphere. During your visit, attend classes or seminars, and talk to the faculty and graduate students. Ask students what they like and dislike about the school. Explore the campus to see if you are comfortable there.

It was not so long ago that you were using self-assessment, research, and questioning others to decide where you wanted to go to graduate school. It is not a surprise that these same elements come into play as you evaluate the colleges where you were accepted.

If you have been selected at several schools, here are six key questions:

1. If all things are equal at the other colleges, consider whether one Ivy League or top school may have a slight edge of prestige and visibility in your chosen field. All such schools have good reputations in general but are almost always slightly better in one field or another. Finding out which one will give your degree more recognition and make you more marketable.

2. Analyze the program to see if it fulfills your own academic and professional objectives. Rankings are admittedly difficult since they are usually based on composite scores covering various factors. Look at performance of alumni on professional licensing exams, research facilities, student services, and other factors to help in creating an overall ranking. Of course, you should also look at the faculty and their scholarly reputation, accessibility to students, and research interests. Keep in mind that the reputation of faculty members rests mainly on published work, which does not directly have any benefit to you as a student.

3. Assess the financial implications of your choice, comparing the costs and benefits. Look at the total costs of pursuing your degree at your various options. When you add up all the costs, ask yourself this basic question: Am I willing to take on the type of debt that may be necessary to help me complete this program?

4. Take a look at the implications, both personal and professional, of your chosen institution. This will vary according to your own situation, of course. If you are a single, 21-year-old, recent college graduate, you will look at this question in an entirely different light than a married mother of two children would look at it. You will have to make this individual evaluation, taking into account your own personal situation. Some considerations include the cost of living in an area; employment opportunities for you and your spouse, if you have one; cultural offerings; and intangible items such as lifestyle. Where do you want to live after school? Generally, it is best to select a college in the same geographic region where you might want to practice a profession or look for employment. You will be establishing valuable contacts throughout your graduate school days that may be of immense help when you complete your degree.

5. Imagine what it would be like working for several years in this particular place with these faculty members and the students here

as your colleagues and friends. This is an area that you can study after a second visit. Look at the level of intellectual stimulation found here. This is important because you will have to maintain motivation for a long time, which is not always an easy job in graduate school. If you have a family, you will want to judge whether you can juggle your student role with family responsibilities and employment. To accomplish that, you should look for flexible programs. You may also want to take a look at services such as childcare and support groups.

6. Finally, develop a backup plan. If the only program that accepts you fails to measure up to your criteria, you are fine because you can put a secondary plan into effect while at the same time finding out what you can do to get admission to your first choice.

Do not be shy about asking for advice. Seek the assistance of a career counselor if you are currently in college. You could also talk with trusted mentors or friends about the pros and cons of each program in comparison to your own needs. Taking the time to thoroughly consider your needs will be a significant aid to helping you make the right choice.

CHAPTER 4

Things to Keep in Mind Throughout the Process

Create an Action Application Schedule

You have almost certainly heard this cliché all your life: It is never too early to . . . well, just about anything. While it is difficult to know where to begin, breaking down your goals can simplify matters. For example, how about these choices: (a) decide on a career; (b) start saving for college or for some other goal; (c) start a timeline to apply to graduate school.

Briefly

Noted

The age of doctorate candidates ranges widely. For example, a study on the distribution of doctorate recipients by age from the National Opinion Research Center shows this breakdown: ages 21 to 25— 286; ages 26 to 30—12,405; ages 31 to 35—11,313; ages 36 to 40—5,612; ages 41 to 45—3,354; and over 45—5,394.

Whether you are in high school or working, you have only a limited time for yourself to do the "fun" things you like such as shopping, seeing a movie, hanging out with friends, or going to concerts and sporting events. Creating a "schedule" does not sound on the surface like it is another word for fun, does it?

While no one wants you to skip a movie and stay home to study all the time, you probably realize by now that it is not easy or simple to get into graduate school. It will take effort, but if you take the attitude that you can find some balance between school, work, and your social life, you can structure your own timeline. A schedule is an important key to your success, and it is not necessarily drudgery. If you take a positive attitude, it can help you learn a lot about yourself, and it can even be fun. Self-examination and finding your strengths and weaknesses is a key element to getting into graduate school. It is never too early to start working on your application process to graduate school because it all starts with your grades as a freshman in high school.

Let us take a look at what you should be doing starting with your freshman year in college. This guideline is general and allows you flexibility when it comes to precise dates, but at the same time, it gives you specific goals that should be met within a time frame. If you are not currently a college student, you can speed up or slow down the process according to your own situation in which you might be working full-time or part-time or facing other circumstances.

Freshman Year

- Begin to narrow down your interests

through coursework, volunteer experience, and experiential learning opportunities. Consider the possibility of job shadowing and interviewing professionals.

- Focus on getting as strong a GPA as you can. Sure, it is early in your educational career, but you might as well find out if your have the right study and personal habits to make high grades. This is a good time to test that out, since your GPA will not be counted as much as in later school years. If you find your grades are not up to your expectations, discovering this early gives you a head start on looking for ways to improve your performance in school.

- Build relationships with faculty and advisors, looking to them for some guidance in achieving your goals.

- If you are not involved in any extracurricular activities, try a few of them. Also consider volunteer work.

Sophomore Year

- Continue to narrow down your specific interests. If you are interested in engineering, for example, try to determine whether you prefer a specific area such as aerospace, chemistry, or electrical engineering.

- Take some of the core math, science, writing, and speech courses. This will help you get some potentially difficult courses out of the way early in your college career.

- Contact a graduate of a department that interests you and interview him or her about advice for preparing for graduate school. Try to find out whether your interviewee thought the school offered a good program (it almost certainly did if it was a top school). Attempt to find out what the experience of attending graduate school here was like. Any in-depth knowledge you can obtain of the graduate school will help you later determine if this is the right place for you.

- Find out more about possible careers of interest to you. If you are in school, visit the institution's career center. Talk to counselors there about getting career experience in your later college years. For those would-be grad students not currently in school, explore the Internet and other sources. The library still has plenty of books and there is more information there than you can find on the Internet.

- During your research, be sure to find out what is practical and what careers will be in demand in the future. For example, aerospace engineers were in high demand during NASA's (National Aeronautical and Space Administration) push to put a man on the moon, but demand quickly tapered off afterwards. In all likelihood, you will not want to choose a career that is on the decline. Bear in mind what happened to buggy whip manufacturers when the Model T Fords first came out in the early part of the 20th century.

- Take time to look into possible volunteer jobs for the summer. Look at opportunities at hospitals or clinics, for example. Concentrate on fields that might be related to your future career. Instead of taking a job selling shoes at the local Macy's, for example, find work that will be helpful when you fill out your application forms for graduate school.

- Consider summer course work, but be mindful that laboratory science courses are often not available at this time. Still, you should be able to find some courses to supplement your regular curriculum.

Junior Year

- Talk to faculty members and more students about graduate programs. Ask them questions and get their recommendations. Interview as many individuals as you can.

- Narrow your choices of graduate programs. This is not an easy job, but it will have to be done at some point. Get started now.

- Write to several schools asking about their programs. Compile information on these schools.

- Try to visit your the schools that interest you the most. This can be expensive, but it will help immensely in your later decisions.

- Prepare a folder for each school, which should contain information such as specific deadlines and other requirements for various programs. Also, your folder should contain other easily accessible information that will help you make decisions later in your college years.

- Write a letter to or e-mail specific people who have published interesting articles and ask about their programs and their current research. This will not only give you an idea of what a school is doing, but it will also be helpful when you are being interviewed by faculty members who will want to know why you chose to apply to their particular program.

- Become involved in a research project with a faculty member. This may not be an easy task, but it will be worth it if you can pull it off. One way to start is to send a letter or e-mail to faculty members after determining what types of projects they are involved in.

- Pick up information about exams and tests

you will have to take. Research them to see how you can better prepare yourself.

- Enlist the help of at least three faculty members to write letters of recommendation. These obviously should be faculty members who know you and have given you good grades.

- Draft a personal statement of your academic and professional goals. This does not have to be complete now, but starting to write it will help you think about it, and you can add more details later.

- Determine the remaining courses to be taken in preparation for any standardized exam you might have to take. For example, you will need to take the MCAT to apply to medical or veterinary school.

Briefly

Noted

"I think the most important thing about graduate school is if you like the environment of the school. That's why visiting is so important. It sounds benign but the environment of the school is a sign of what it is like and the kind of students who are attracted by it," according to graduate degree holder Caleb John Clark who says he has "squeaked and wriggled [his] way into graduate school three times in the last seven years." He has a master's degree in educational technology from San Diego State University.

Senior Year (Fall Semester)

- You should have already have taken the GRE exams or schedule taking it this semester. Do not delay because time passes quickly when you are a senior and involved in the usual round of grades and graduation in addition to taking steps for what you will do in the future.

- Check to see if you are satisfied with your score at this time because application deadlines will begin soon and continue on through next year. Remember that some schools will not accept late test scores.

- If you have letters of recommendation by now, thank the writers for their assistance and support. This is a step many students overlook because of the many details of applying to graduate school. This will help in the future and it is simple courtesy.

- Consider doing a chart of all the schools where you have applied. This should include vital information such as application deadlines, anticipated acceptance dates, and practical matters such as what types of financial aid are available. Such a chart will help when you are attempting to make your final decision.

- It is time to fill out your applications, write your personal statements, and be sure you have your letters of recommendation at hand.

- Share your personal statement with professors you know to get their thoughts on the subject. This will help you enhance your statement, which is a critical area often neglected by students who are reluctant to write about themselves.

- Order your transcripts.

- Download and complete drafts of your application forms. Review and edit your answers.

- Submit your completed application forms.

- Develop a backup plan in case you are not admitted to your first choice.

- You have a lot to do this semester to prepare your graduate application forms, so if possible you might consider taking a lighter course load.

Senior Year (Spring Semester)

- Follow up to make sure any documents you sent out have been received.

- Revise your personal statement. You have already discussed it with your professors, so you can edit it with their opinions in mind.

- Assuming you have done the proper planning (and followed your schedule), this is the semester you will be making decisions and evaluating offers. This is a good time to review your organized list of graduate schools to see what the major differences are in the courses offered and other critical information.

- File your Free Application for Federal Student Aid (FAFSA) form to apply for financial aid. Even if you receive other funding and do not need it, it is good to have this option.

- Now is an excellent time to enlist some help. Look for friends, other students, family, faculty, and others to help in your decisions.

- Replies from graduate schools should come in by April. Call schools to check the status of your application if they have not replied by April 15.

- Throughout your undergraduate days, research and read professional publications in your field of interest.

Briefly

Noted

An applicant to a research-oriented clinical psychology program may be rejected because he or she did not read the program materials carefully. He or she may have professed an interest in practical therapy — obviously not a good fit for a research-oriented program.

Something else to consider in your planning process is the importance of getting relevant work experience in your field. This should be done as early as possible. One major reason for looking early is that you might not find immediate opportunities. Another reason is that you might be lucky enough to find something now and discover another type of work later. This will give you even more experience and add another possible letter of recommendation from someone who can testify as to how your good work ethic would meet graduate school standards. Even if you are a senior in high school and still have not found some work experience, do not panic. You may still have time. The point here is to look as early as possible so you do not miss out.

Do not overlook other experiences related to your field that are helpful in getting into graduate school. For example, whether you are a freshman or a senior, you can make it a habit to attend events hosted by your department such as talks by special guest lecturers. You will learn something interesting that you did not know before, and gain some insight into possible careers. The faculty attending these events will also notice your repeated appearance, and will view you as a dedicated student with an intense interest in the field.

In many graduate programs, relevant work experience is one of the most important nonobjective criteria for acceptance by admissions committees.

Practice, Practice, Practice: Taking Graduate Record Exams and Other Tests

If you are like most people, the thought of taking a test is scary. Perhaps even the thought of it makes your heart beat faster. Your breathing becomes labored. You may sweat or even suffer from headaches or have an upset stomach. If it is any consolation, this is normal. For many students, the scariest part of applying to graduate school is taking the Graduate Record Examination General Test or GRE.

In many cases, when we are afraid, we practice avoidance. If you are fearful of water, you do not go in the swimming pool, for example. But when it comes to the GRE, there is no way to avoid it. Virtually all graduate programs require that you take either the GRE or other professional tests. If you are thinking maybe you can cheat on the system, possibly by sending in a "fake score," forget it. Scores are sent directly to admissions offices. You may also have to take a GRE Subject Test in your field.

First find out exactly what tests you have to take. Contact the Educational Testing Service, which administers the GRE and GMAT (Graduate Management Admission Test). The LSAT is given by the Law School Admission Council, while the MCAT is administered by the Association of American Medical Colleges.

The more you know about these tests, the more confidence you will have. The GRE tests your knowledge and skills in three areas: verbal, quantitative, and analytical writing. It should be comforting to know that the verbal and quantitative sections are similar to a test you have already taken: the SAT you took to get into college. The verbal sections test your reading comprehension and the quantitative sections tests your high school math. The analytical writing section consists of two, timed essays: one requires you to express and support a position on a given issue, and the other tests your logic for a given argument.

Preparing for your GRE is different from when you were an undergraduate. Most of the tests involve a series of strictly timed sections. This puts a lot of pressure on the test taker. There is a strong connection between test scores and how many questions in each section you are able to complete without guessing or running out of time. Does this seem obvious? Not entirely because it suggests that the best strategy for taking the test is to be prepared. The best way to prepare is to spend as much time as you can practicing and interpreting test instructions or questions. A good strategy is to write at least one practice a week.

Not everyone places a lot of stock in GRE scores. Some programs consider it important, but others do not have a high regard for it. Some schools focus on all three elements, while others only look at two. The obvious way to find out how each program views the test is to ask.

It is important to find out which tests you will have to take long before you apply to graduate school. There are several reasons why, including the fact that most tests are only given on a few specific days of the year. You must also allow time for the results to be processed and mailed by their application deadlines to the programs where you have applied. It takes more than a month for the testing service to process and send out your official scores.

You must register for the test in advance, often a minimum of several weeks prior to the date you want to take the test. You will have to pay a minimum fee. There are provisions for taking tests at an earlier time if you are willing to pay a late registration fee.

CASE STUDY: CALEB JOHN CLARK

Caleb John Clark, whose scores were so low someone recommended he be tested for a learning disability, studied the Princeton Review and hired a tutor. "I could have probably studied more, as in several months versus one month, and done better. Practice tests seem to do the trick," he says.

If you are applying to graduate school within two years of undergraduate work, take the GRE soon. Studies have shown that performance on standardized tests decline with each year you are out of school. Scores are good for a few years, so a test taken during or immediately after undergraduate school does not have to be used immediately. Some graduate programs accept scores up to five years old, but you should check to be sure.

For most students, it is a good idea to take any tests

at least a year before applying to graduate school. The reason is that, if you do poorly on the tests, you will have time to do it again, this time with better preparation. There is another reason to take the tests well before applying. Taking the tests at the last minute when you are busy scurrying around to meet all the application requirements makes it harder for you to perform well. There is often not a lot of time to study when you are busy getting letters of recommendation, filling out application forms, writing personal statements, and doing other things necessary to complete the work to get into grad school.

There is also a psychological advantage to taking tests early. Some people feel less pressure knowing that they have time to take the tests again if they wish. That fact could even enhance your test performance.

So you know what tests you have to take. Here is the best way to avoid test stress, and this cannot be repeated too often: be prepared. Familiarize yourself with the types of questions you will be asked before the exam. The more prepared you are, the better you will do.

You should at least buy practice test books for the GRE General Test or the subject tests from the Educational Testing Service. Several organizations, including the Princeton Review and the Kaplan organization, offer classes to help you prepare for the tests. Costs can be in the thousands, so you will have to determine if you can afford it.

Here are some other strategies for making you more confident when you take your tests:

- Get to the exam room a few minutes early to familiarize yourself with the environment. Set out your supplies beforehand. Take a deep breath.

- When the test starts, read the instructions at least twice. Be sure you understand the instructions even if it takes a third reading. Many students miss getting the correct answers because they misunderstand what is being asked.

- If you do not understand something, do not ignore it and go ahead with the test. Ask the proctor as soon as possible.

- If you have to write an essay, do not immediately start, but take a few minutes to organize your thoughts and write a brief outline. Do not start writing without an outline first. If you immediately start writing, chances are you will be halfway through when you think of a better way to express yourself. By that time it is too late because you have gone off in another direction.

- Work steadily and do not speed up even when time starts to run out. Read carefully without worrying too much about the time.

Briefly

Noted

"Success on the GRE is a critical element in the graduate school admissions process. Not only will a high score help you get into one of your top-choice schools, scores are also used to determine eligibility for merit-based fellowships as well as teaching and research assistantships," according to Kaplan, an educational company that attempts to help individuals achieve their educational and career goals, (a wholly owned subsidiary of the Washington Post Company).

Here are a handful of test preparation resources:

Recommended books, most of which have real tests to practice on:

- *The Best Test Preparation for the GRE General Test*, Research and Education Association. Piscataway, New Jersey.

- *Cracking the GRE*, Adam Robinson. Random House, New York

- *Practicing to Take the GRE General Test — Big Book*, The Educational Testing Service. Warner Books, New York

- *Princeton Review: Inside the GRE*, the Princeton Review. Random House, New York

Kaplan, Inc. and the Princeton Review are among the dozens of companies who offer preparation courses for the GRE and other tests.

A little stress at this time it not a necessarily bad thing. It will help keep you alert and probably improve your performance. You do not want to be too relaxed, but at the same time, you do not want to let your natural anxiety hamper your performance. You have heard it before, but it bears repeating: In tests, as in life itself, some balance is always necessary.

Meeting Deadlines and Other Timely Matters

The most important four words about deadlines are: Do not miss them. Most programs strictly adhere to their deadlines and if you miss one, forget it. You are out. Some schools will give preference to complete applications meeting the deadline and accept applications as long as space is available. Even if you are applying to a program that allows some leeway, perhaps a few days or even a week or two past the published deadline, you should not fail to get everything in on time. You often do not know which schools have some flexibility, and being late leaves a bad impression.

Before we get into the important subject of deadlines, consider another timing issue: What is the best timing for going to graduate schools? For some, it may be never, but perhaps you have already decided that grad school is for you.

One good point to consider when looking at the timing of getting your master's degree is that its value goes down the longer you wait to get it. At the beginning of your career, you can get a jump on others with a master's degree from a top or Ivy League school. In the middle of your career, that jump no longer applies, so the value declines. Many large companies want to see a master's degree before you move into the top levels of management. It used to be that business schools often encouraged candidates to wait a few years before applying. But that schedule does not make sense for women who want children and careers.

The best time to go to graduate school is when you have a clear plan and you are sure of what you want to do. If you spend the time and money to get a degree, and then determine you are interested in another field, you have wasted a critical early stage of your career.

Do some practical thinking on your timing. If you are right out of college and determined to teach at the higher levels of academia, keep in mind that getting a tenure track job in some fields — the humanities immediately comes to mind — is virtually impossible because of a lack of demand.

Admissions officers sometimes complain that students often do not allow themselves enough time and then expect to receive special consideration. From the school's standpoint, deadlines for graduate applications generally come near the end of the fall term in December; however, each school has different application deadlines.

Starting early usually means beginning your graduate school search at the end of the summer or the beginning of the fall term the year before you wish to attend graduate school. Successfully navigating this task will require your efforts throughout the term.

One major reason for meeting deadlines early is that if you apply early, you can wait patiently to receive confirmation that everything is in order. If, for some reason, a standardized test score or a transcript is not processed, you will still have time to correct the problem prior to the deadline.

If you beat an application deadline by a few weeks, you are less likely to be forced into rushing around at the last minute. This can detract from the quality of your application. Admissions committees also take note when it appears that a student's application forms are disorganized and not done properly.

Graduate program directors and their staff do not like it when students call or drop by on the application deadline date. On the other hand, admissions officials notice if you beat their deadlines. You appear to them to be organized. You also make an impression on admissions officials as being enthusiastic. Some programs begin reviewing applications before the deadline, even though most of them have not yet arrived. Application files that are received early may receive a more careful evaluation. Hopefully, the more closely your application is evaluated, the more it will stand out from the crowd.

Early on in the process, you should sit down and write a plan of action. This does not have to be a lengthy multi-page document, but more a list of points outlining what you want to accomplish at certain times during the process. This is only emulating what virtually all successful people do — they have a plan.

In addition to helping you stay on top of what you have to do, this plan forces you to think specifically about the steps you will need to accomplish and when you need to have those steps completed. This is far from listing everything you need to have done. It is just a guideline, but one that will keep you on track. It is not an exact plan; it is flexible enough so that you can make changes as you go along.

When do you start some sort of schedule? Ideally, when you start undergraduate school, though few can boast they began that early.

The key to getting everything in on time with a minimum of stress is to begin early. Begin to take the necessary steps well before the application deadline. Students often underestimate the time needed to properly fill out application forms and take the other necessary steps. You will need to make arrangements for transcripts and letters and other materials to be sent several weeks prior to deadlines.

It is also important to leave extra time in case any of the offices responsible for processing your request make errors or are delayed due to technical problems. Transcripts can be misplaced and even the post office can make mistakes that lead to costly delays in your admission forms.

Exactly how you do it is up to you; but create some kind of filing system or checklist to keep track of when you need to supply different pieces of your application package such as transcripts or letters of recommendation. Use the checklist to follow up to make sure that all of your materials are being submitted on time. Write down important dates.

Programs vary a great deal in how long they take to get back to you. Some programs wait until all of the various components of your application have arrived; others handle it in a more piecemeal fashion. Be sure to make photocopies of everything you send just in case there is a breakdown and some materials do not get through.

Because some programs do not inform students that their applications have been received, you might need to follow up on your own. Make telephone calls if necessary to ensure everything is in order. Write down your actions on your checklist as you go along to keep a written account of what you have done and when you did it.

How long should you wait before calling? Your application form and your personal statement or essays may be the only parts of your application that you have direct responsibility for putting in the mail, though there are exceptions for programs that require you to collect your letters of recommendation and send them along with the application form. Expect it to take up to two weeks for your school to process your request for standardized test scores and send them to the various graduate programs.

How long will it take you to get out of graduate school? The answer, of course, is that it depends. Your master's degree could take anywhere from one to three years (most often, two), depending on the field. It also depends on whether or not you have write a thesis, which often takes a lot of time. A Ph.D. takes longer. The time required depends largely on the area of study.

Briefly

Noted

The median time to get a Ph.D. in history is 8.3 years or 6.1 in the sciences, according to In Pursuit of the Ph.D. *by Bowen and Rudenstine.*

Exactly how much time you need to spend on preparing yourself for graduate school is something you will have to decide but remember that it is likely you will not have to worry about spending too much time. You can never be too prepared. So expect and budget a lot of hours toward preparing your application.

Ghostwriting: Drafting Highly Effective Reference Letters

You got straight As in college. You scored well on all

your tests. So getting letters of recommendation written is no big deal, right? Wrong. Imagine you take a casual approach to enlisting faculty members to write your letters. Perhaps all they say is that you received straight A grades. That is not what you want. Faculty members have to know you to write effective letters. They also have to think highly of you. Letters will be much stronger if the writers can make specific comments on how enthusiastic you are or cite particular excellent papers or your stimulating participation in class.

A well-written letter of recommendation provides the admissions committee with information that is not found anywhere else in the application package. A letter of recommendation is a detailed communication from a faculty member about the personal qualities, accomplishments, and experiences that make you unique and perfect for the program where you have applied. Letters of recommendation are basically similar to celebrity endorsements, but since they do not come from celebrities, they have to substitute substance for sizzle.

Letters of recommendation are required for acceptance to the vast majority of graduate degree programs. They usually ask for three letters. Who you choose to write these letters is obviously an important decision. If you have a famous professor, it is helpful to ask him or her to write a letter for you. An admissions committee cannot help but be impressed by your name dropping in this case. Most of you will probably not have access to that type of person. When seeking letters of recommendation, you immediately face three questions: who to ask, when to ask, and how to ask.

Who to Ask

For academic applications, letters from teachers or professors are generally preferable to letters from employers. Admissions officers are looking to supplement their knowledge of your academic performance and aptitude with concrete evidence that you are a dedicated and enthusiastic learner. Most schools recognize the value of a dynamic, diverse student body and are usually eager to fill their spots with candidates who have been actively engaged in both academic and extracurricular activities. These letters should reflect not only your participation and performance in the classroom, but also your initiative outside of class. That can range from research projects done with your professors through leadership in group activities and active contributions to classroom discussions.

Ideally, people who write letters for you should:

- Know your work

- Have a high opinion of you

- Know where you are applying

- Know you well enough to write with expertise

- Be aware of your educational and career goals

- Be able to favorably compare you with your peers

- Testify to your aptitude, curiosity, and industriousness

- Demonstrate your maturity and seriousness of purpose

- Portray you as a leader

- Paint you as "well rounded"

- Compliment your character

- Include other favorable information about you — things not readily apparent from test scores or transcripts

- Know you well enough not only to describe your personality and major points, but also to include personal anecdotes in the letter

- Have the highest or most relevant job title

- Be comfortable writing a letter for you

- Have prior experience in writing letters of recommendation

- Write well

When to Ask

The more time you can give someone who is writing letter for you, the better. First consider the date when the letter has to be received. Remember that professors are busy with preparing lessons, conducting research, correcting papers, and even writing letters of recommendation. As you are aware of the deadline for receiving the letter, it is important to give professors plenty of time. Even if you find someone at the last minute, be mindful that he or she would be hard-pressed to take the time to write a glowing letter of recommendation. Also consider another reality — you may be only one of many students seeking these letters. For all of these reasons, it is important to give professors ample time to write the letter of recommendation. If possible, ask them early in the semester (at least two months in advance), before they are consumed with correcting midterm and final exams. If that time frame is not practical, try at least a month in advance.

How to Ask

Asking someone to write a letter of recommendation for you is a personal request. You should make every effort to have a face-to-face appointment with your letter writers. Try to avoid asking for a letter of recommendation via e-mail. You should make in-person appointments with would-be writers for several reasons:

1. You should be able to gauge whether or not your recommender is enthusiastic about writing you

a letter. At the same time, this is the time to ask whether or not they feel comfortable enough in writing you a strong letter of recommendation. If you sense any hesitation on their part or they are in any way ambiguous in their reply, hear them out, thank them, and prepare to find an alternative.

2. An in-person meeting allows you to articulate more thoroughly why you want to attend graduate school, and gives you the chance to spell out your future goals.

3. One by-product of the in-person appointment is access to information about the programs you may not be familiar with. Many students forget that their professors have colleagues at the institutions and programs to which they are applying. They may have similar research interests and may have even collaborated on projects or experiments. If you use the opportunity to discuss your graduate school choices along with your request for a letter, most professors will be receptive and may be even more enthusiastic because your program is one of special interest to them.

If you have no choice and must send a letter or e-mail, here is a sample of what you might say:

Sample Letters

Dear Dr. Everett,

As you may know, I am applying to graduate school at Yale University, and I am writing to ask if you would provide me with a supportive letter of recommendation. The application deadline for the college is February 15. I have enclosed a recommendation form required by each application and a signed a waiver indicating that I surrender my right to see the letter at any time.

The directions for each application indicate that I may enclose sealed letters of recommendation with my mailed applications. If you are not comfortable with enclosing your letter of recommendation in a sealed envelope and letting me mail it with my other application materials, please let me know. In the latter case, I will provide you with an addressed, stamped envelope so the letters of recommendation can be submitted to the college.

As you may recall, I have taken two courses with you: Early Childhood Education and Child Counseling, an Introduction. Each course led to my earning an A. I wrote my ten-page final paper on "The Impact of Freudian Psychology on Early Education Initiatives." Currently, my GPA is 3.57.

Enclosed is a copy of my résumé so you can see the extracurricular activities I have been involved in and the work experience I have amassed during my four years here. My part-time work as a Behavioral Specialist for Atlantic Home Health Services has given me useful direct-service experience. My clients have included children, ages 7 to 12, suffering from autism, and mild mental retardation. Working one-to-one with these children has given me the opportunity to move from theory to practice with the concepts I learned in your courses.

Also enclosed is one paper I wrote for you (and your thoughtful comments).

Thank your for considering my request for a letter of recommendation. If you would like further information, please feel welcome to contact me at 450-335-8190 or JWakefield@aol.

The best thing that you can do to ensure that your letters cover all the bases is to provide your referees with all the necessary information. Do not assume they will remember anything about you. We all think we are memorable and unique, but professors cannot keep track of hundreds of students each semester. Include resumés and, if possible, papers you have written, especially if they are brief and do not require a lot of time for the professor to read.

There are some key issues that you should be

communicating to your letter writers. You should tell them what kind of graduate study interests you, what drew you to this field, and the activities you were involved in that contribute to your interest or prepare you to pursue it further.

A résumé or CV helps your letter writers to know more about you and your experiences outside of the classroom. A résumé will also outline your internships.

Another important component of your package to a letter writer should be a copy of your transcript; and unofficial copy, in this case, is all right. This provides additional information about your academic preparation and achievement. If you have any concerns about your overall academic work — perhaps you think it does not reflect your true ability — your professor may be able to write something on the positive side. Bring this up in a discussion or mention it in a letter. If there are other potential negatives, you should also raise those issues. Perhaps you had family responsibilities that kept you from studying more to achieve higher grades, for example. Look carefully at your letter to see if there are any negative issues that have yet to be explained. If there are any negatives at all, do not gloss over them. Address these issues in the same way a lawyer would in a rebuttal of someone else's argument. Explain the situation and give reasons. Do not whine or complain, or worst of all, ignore the issue.

In addition to making these points in a letter, be sure to tell the recommender why you have chosen them. This is certain to be a question they will ask. Your answer will help your recommender understand how your mind works, and it will help the letter writer in deciding what he or she will want to say.

Now you have some strong, well-written letters of recommendation, but your job still is not done. As the application deadline approaches, check back with your referees to ensure the letters were sent on time. You will receive a better response if you do not nag them by repeated calls or contacts.

A thoughtful and considerate thank you note recognizes the time and effort your recommenders put forth on your behalf, and goes a long way in keeping you in their good graces should you need another recommendation at a later date. Also, it is simply good manners.

Here is an example of a positive letter of recommendation:

Dear ------

As the Dean of ABC College, I have had the pleasure of knowing Emily Acer for the last four years. She has been a tremendous student and an asset to our school. I would like to highly recommend Sally for your graduate program.

I feel confident that Emily will continue to succeed in her studies. She is a dedicated student and, thus far, her grades have been exemplary. She has compiled an almost perfect record with a 3.9 GPA. In class, she has proven to be a take-charge person who is able to successfully develop plans and implement them.

Emily has also assisted us in our admissions office. She has successfully demonstrated leadership ability by counseling new and prospective students. Her advice has been a great help to these students, many of whom have taken time to share their comments with me regarding her pleasant and encouraging attitude.

While a student here, Emily was employed in various positions, including teaching a museum program to fourth-grade classes in the ABC School District, teaching both adults and children to ride horses, and managing horse show participation for a local riding stable. She accomplished all these tasks with great initiative and with a very positive attitude.

Emily has a wonderful rapport with people of all ages, especially the "at-risk" children she worked with at the ABC School and the ABC Child and Family Center. Sally has a special talent working with the children who need more guidance and support than those typically found in a traditional classroom setting.

Her ability to connect with her students and her talent at teaching simple concepts, as well as more advanced topics, are both truly superior.

It is for these reasons that I highly recommend Emily without reservations. Her drive and abilities will be an asset to your establishment. If you have any questions regarding this recommendation, please do not hesitate to contact me.

David DuChamp
Dean
ABC College

You can see the components that go into making this an outstanding letter. The writer covers a student's academic career, and puts it in the best light. The writer also gets into the student's outside activities, often in specific terms that show her success. The writer has conveyed a sense of the qualities that will emerge to make this student successful in graduate school.

Writing Compelling Statements of Purpose, Letters of Intent, and Essays

Not all graduate programs require a statement of purpose, and some programs have a different word for it, such as a letter of intent, biographical essay, or career goal statement. Whatever you call it, this is perhaps the most difficult piece of writing you will do.

That should not discourage you, however, because once you understand what is involved and the purpose, you will be able to write a compelling piece that could vastly improve your chances of acceptance.

One goal of a statement of purpose is to describe your own hopes and aspirations. That is the easy part. The tricky part comes when you have to apply your aspirations to your proposed career. Generally, admissions officers are far less interested in your qualifications than they are in whether or not your goals are realistic and whether you are accurately imagining your career once you are accepted into a graduate program.

Does the difference between being rejected or accepted rely on a personal statement? The answer is yes, sometimes it does. There have been cases where admissions committees put less weight on test scores and GPAs to accept students who clearly communicated how they fit into their chosen field and how that field fit their lives. A weak statement can derail even good candidates. Many students do not take this statement seriously enough. Many students think it will take them a few hours to craft a good statement, when they should be thinking in terms of several days or even a few weeks.

Some colleges ask for open-ended personal statements such as "tell us something about yourself." Graduate students often groan over that one because it does not give them any idea what the admissions committee wants to know.

Briefly Noted

Here is how Yale University describes what they want from a Personal Statement of Purpose: "A 500–1000 word statement concerning your past work, preparation for the intended field of study, relevant background and interests, academic plans, and career objectives is required. It should be used to describe your reasons for applying to the particular Yale department or program. This statement may assist the admissions committee in evaluating your aptitude and motivation for graduate study."

What is the admissions committee looking for in a statement of purpose? You have two goals: to be persuasive and to be personal. Your statement should demonstrate how right you are for the program, and how the program fits into your life. Anything that furthers that notion should be considered as pertinent material.

You are not writing a comprehensive biography, but look for areas of your life that dovetail into your proposed program. This gives you the chance to demonstrate that you understand the program by citing relevant experience. Do not be afraid to get personal. You want to be honest about yourself and your goals.

Be mindful that "persuasive" and "personal" are not mutually exclusive; they are qualities you can show at the same time. If you are entering some programs such as scientific-based areas, you might want to skew your response on the side of reason. If you are looking at arts and literature, you almost certainly have more room for creativity. You can veer away from an emphasis on professional qualifications and show more of how your particular mind functions.

Do not start your essay at the last minute. Instead, spend a few months thinking about what you are going to say. Do not be afraid to rewrite, either. You should plan on doing several drafts.

After you have written the first, second, or third draft, here are some criteria to evaluate whether you are on the right track:

- Does the first paragraph capture your attention?

- Have you answered all the questions thoroughly?

- Has anything relevant been omitted? Perhaps your work or academic experience has not been fully covered.

- How about your character: Does your essay reflect favorably on your own character traits?

- Is your essay well-written?

- Is the grammar, tone, and verb agreement perfect?

By now, you have done your homework about a department's faculty. If the situation arises where a certain faculty member strikes you as someone you might be interested in working with, say so in your essay. Be concise but specific about why you chose this person. Do not view this as a way of courting favor with the admissions committee. Only do this if you are being honest. If you are being dishonest, or there is any reason for the admissions committee's to believe you are being dishonest, it could cost you dearly.

In composing your essay, try to empathize with the admissions committee. Consider what they want to know about you, such as: What sets you apart from other applicants applying for the same program? They want information on why you are interested in this field and the depth of your understanding regarding the demands of this field.

Admissions committee members will also be interested in what prompted you to move into this field, and want specific details on your career aspirations. Avoid generalizations when addressing this topic — think specifics. If there are any gaps or discrepancies in your academic record, this is a perfect time to address them. The committee wants to know details about the skills and personal characteristics that enhance your chances of success. The ultimate question is: Have you given the committee enough reasons to be interested in you?

Here are some areas to reflect on when you consider what to write about:

Everyone loves a story. Can you tell a story about yourself? In your story, cite specific past experiences that made you interested in your chosen career path. Include personal information to make your story interesting and believable. Tell anecdotes. Too often, students make sweeping generalizations that turn out to be boring and flat. You want some juice in your statement.

How do you determine what aspects of your personal life are important? Consider what is special about you. Did you have to overcome obstacles or special hardships to get where you are today? Ask yourself why, how, and when you became interested in your chosen field? What has happened since to make you even more certain that you are on the right path? What particular skills and characteristics do you possess that will make you successful in graduate school?

Summing Up: Some Dos and Don'ts

Some Dos:

- Do start early. Leave yourself plenty of time to revise, record, and rewrite. You can always improve your presentation.

- Do read the directions carefully. You will want to answer the questions as directly as possible, and you will want to adhere to word limits. Express yourself as briefly and as clearly as you can.

- Tell the truth about yourself. You are completely unknown to the admissions committee.

- Be specific about what this particular school can do for you.

- Focus on aspects of yourself that will show your best and most praiseworthy traits.

- If you have overcome some adversity, worked through a difficult project, or profited from a specific incident, mention it. Do it in a modest way without appearing to be bragging.

- Remember that a narrow focus is more interesting than broad-based generalizations.

- Short anecdotes about you are always interesting and are far more believable than general statements such as "I am honest and trustworthy." Instead of saying you have those traits, tell of an incident or case history where you showed admirable traits.

- Always write positively. Negatives are not needed.

- Write about your own anxieties. Everybody is human. Admissions committee members have been in this position themselves, so they know what it is like. You will gain points for recognizing your fears and facing up to them.

- Find some ways to relate yourself to the college.

- Tailor your essay for different colleges.

- Be proud. Write about your greatest assets and achievements.

Some Don'ts

- Do not repeat information given elsewhere on your application. Your committee has already seen it. They do not want a repeat.

- Do not use clichés. They are meaningless and will not help your case.

- Do not write on general and sometimes impersonal topics such as your love of peace or the importance of good ethics in American corporations. The college wants to find out about you, and your essay should focus on that rather than your opinions on other subjects.

- Do not try to use this essay to explain shortcomings you think you have, and do not make lengthy and feeble excuses. Be straightforward and explain why you have gotten low scores on some tests, or had a GPA beneath what you are able to do.

- Do not sound too opinionated or express a

know-it-all attitude. Remember that you are a student and are interested in learning what you do not already know.

How do you tell the difference between writing that tells and writing that shows? It is obvious. Consider this statement that comes from a real student: "If it were not for an emphasis on morals, instilled in me by family members, and their strong support system, I would not be where I am today." This is a weak and clichéd statement that tells the admission committee nothing. Substitute something like this: "My grandparents were so poor they did not have a car, or a dishwasher, or even modern conveniences such as a clothes dryer. We often walked to our destinations and my grandmother hung out the wash to dry almost every day. Going without things as we did taught me some important lessons. My grandmother made the most of what she had. She was well-known and respected. Even at an early age, I recognized the value she placed on maximizing her resources. It was a lesson I have never forgotten and it has served me well throughout my academic career and indeed, my everyday life." This is strong and vivid, and readers will remember it.

Many students think it is important to include facts that are irrelevant to the admissions committee. For example, a student who mentions that he obtained an A in every high school class while also serving as captain of the football team creates the impression you do not know the difference between relevant and irrelevant information. High school is in the distant past. A list of your grades is not important, even if you have a positive grade point average. If you can tie your grades into mentioning certain classes that are relevant to your application, that is not only acceptable but laudatory because admission committee members want to know more about how your efforts mesh with your proposed program.

Some students think they need to get into controversial subjects, but the best advice is to avoid politics and anything about your own political biases. The same principle applies to religion.

On a practical note, be sure in your essay that your grammar and spelling are perfect. You do not want the admissions committees to think you are deficient in grammar.

Try to be as original as possible. Avoid clichés. Write a statement that you think will grab readers and make them interested in your life and experiences.

Show a draft of your personal statement to a friend or a professor who knows you well. Ask for feedback. Do not forget to rewrite as many times as is necessary until you feel that your essay is perfect.

CHAPTER 5

Choosing Samples of Your Work to Submit

L et us say you are applying to the prestigious Graduate School of Journalism at the University of California, Berkeley. You are familiar by now with all the application forms and test scores and letters of recommendation, and all the other various paraphernalia associated with applying to graduate school. The school has information on your proposed degree program, and a wealth of personal information and background that you have provided.

The writing required to get into the journalism graduate program is about as all-encompassing as anywhere. You will have to provide a personal statement, a statement of purpose (750-word limit), a personal history statement (750-word limit), and three samples of professional work. "We expect journalists to be sensitive to language and to organize their thoughts clearly and coherently," says the school's Web site. They ask for only three samples and limit each one to five pages or less; excerpts of longer pieces are acceptable. Two of the three samples must involve writing, but students can also substitute a DVD, a Web site, a documentary, or even a photograph.

The distinctive aspect of these requirements is that they are *specific*. Not all graduate school requirements will be as specific, but these guidelines still leave you, the would-be graduate student, with a choice. What kind of work samples should you submit?

How important are work samples? You cannot exaggerate their importance.

Samples of your work provide the admissions committee with a good idea of your potential. The importance of work can outweigh your college grades. Many programs point out that samples of a student's work are more indicative than grades in predicting how he or she will do in graduate school. Programs will accept a manuscript, an abstract from a scientific meeting, a paper written for a class, or even a report from an independent study. If you are applying to a journalism school, it is obvious that your paper should include stories. If you are applying to a scientific program, you want to provide examples of research even if that work is done in another field. If you do not have sample research, this is a good time to consider some independent research. Admissions committees will applaud your initiative, and it is a good strategy for overcoming low grades.

If there is something that you feel will strengthen your chances, submit it, even if the committee did not ask for it. Students sometimes fear, often rightfully, that they will overwhelm the committee with paper. But if what you are submitting is truly *useful and pertinent,* do not hesitate to pass it on. Of course, that does not mean you send in a crate full of material. If you send in too much material, the committee might not pay attention to any of it. If you do have a lot of material, it is a good idea to condense as much of it as you can and indicate that longer versions are available upon request. Keep a copy of anything you submit because some programs do not return materials as part of the application process.

When it comes to work samples, the more recent the better. It goes without staying that you want to send in your very best work. As you write about your work emphasize your strong research and your writing skills. If you encountered any adversity in your work, it should also be included. Committee members do not want to necessarily know how much you know; they are far more interested in what you have done and how you have accomplished it.

Much of what you read in Chapter 4 on how to write good essays also applies when you select your work samples. This is a professional statement and not a personal one. You should be specific and give details. The entire tone should be respectful, professional, and fairly serious. If possible, identify commonalities in your work samples with ongoing work at the college where you are applying.

Good writing, as you have read in previous chapters, also involves a catchy or attention-grabbing first sentence. You want to have the admissions committee's attention so they are encouraged to read further. Make sure you have a compelling first sentence or two. Admissions committee members are forced to do a lot of reading, so make it easier for them by submitting something they will want to read and not something such as a paper on "how I spent my favorite summer."

What are some common mistakes? Modifying your writing style to pander to admissions committee members or devising something you think they want is one mistake Write about yourself and your experiences. While it is good to point out areas where you showed problem-solving skills, do not dwell on crises or over over-dramatize your work. Going off in widely scattered directions is another common fault. Stick to the point. Keep it factual.

In citing your work experiences, do not be afraid to write about some of your failures. Obviously, you do not want to be negative, but admissions committee members appreciate candor. No one expects all experiences to be positive. Failure is also a growth experience. Many people are convinced that the pillars of success are built on the steps of failure.

Briefly

Noted

"If you can keep your head when all about you are losing theirs and blaming it on you . . . If you can meet with triumph and disaster and treat those two impostors just the same . . . yours is the Earth and everything that's in it."

Rudyard Kipling

Before submitting your work samples, take a few simple steps to polish your effort. Typos and spelling mistakes are unforgivable — proofread carefully. Whenever possible, show what you have done instead of telling about it. Use anecdotes if possible. Always have a trusted faculty member — perhaps your advisor – give you some feedback before doing one final revision.

Diversity, Disabilities, and Affirmative Action

After a decline in the number of minorities applying to graduate school in the 1990s, minority enrollment throughout the last decade have been rising. Women have been applying in record numbers in recent years. African-American, Hispanic, Asian, and Native-American enrollment have also increased substantially. In fact, one in five of all doctoral degrees during a recent year— the largest percentage ever — went to members of a racial or ethnic minority group, according to the National Opinion Research Center.

The U.S. Supreme Court's decision that universities may use race as one factor in admission has helped implement this trend. While most schools now claim they are looking for all types of students, this is not always an authentic claim. If you are a minority, there is a simple way to test the truth: Ask for hard statistics on students' ethnic backgrounds.

Why has diversity emerged in recent years as one of the

top goals at many Ivy League and top graduate schools? Government action is one reason, but graduate schools have started to see the value in a diverse population of students who help create a stimulating educational environment. More and more colleges have launched various efforts to boost minority enrollment. These efforts include offering scholarships, direct mailings, and hiring minority members. If you are a minority, check with your top schools of interest to see what kind of incentives they offer.

Do not be totally swayed or immediately apply to the schools you think offer the most generous programs. Consider other factors such as courses offered and even lifestyle. Why do you need to consider these elements? One reason is that you want to work with the schools that are the most helpful to minorities or are seeking the widest diversity possible.

Students often rely too heavily on information provided directly by graduate schools. This is valuable and, indeed, vital, but students can benefit from getting information from other students with firsthand experience. Most colleges have graduate student associations; some even have associations for minority students. Other groups that may be of help include graduate conferences, seminars, and minority graduate meetings. The U.S. Department of Education sponsors Trio Programs, which are educational outreach programs to motivate and support students from disadvantaged backgrounds. Many of their employees have been through graduate programs themselves and can be valuable sources of information.

Because you are a minority, your focus on finding information is somewhat different from other students. You will want to track down information that applies to you. Instead of finding out the general graduation, for example, you will want to see how minorities are faring in completing their course of study.

Some students try to shy away from race, but that is not a good idea. In your personal statement and on-campus interview, do not be reluctant to bring up the subject — it will not go away. You do not have to raise the issue out of the blue, but when it does come up, address it squarely.

Perhaps because of all the publicity given affirmative action, some students think the best schools will court them despite low grades or poor test scores. There is no automatic exception for minorities, but they do sometimes have access to resources not open to everyone. Numerous individuals and organizations focus on graduate opportunities and financial aid for minority students. Some examples include the McKnight Foundation, the Gem Program, and the Chancellor's Graduate Fellowship Program for African Americans at Washington University.

Schools have made progress toward finding ways of recruiting minorities, so as a student, you will find typical on-campus events might be geared toward you as a minority. Schools sometimes pay for all travel, lodging, and even food expenses as part of a school program. Some schools also have faculty members who have been appointed by their department or program to act as a resource for minorities. Check out Web sites as well. They sometimes have application tips specifically geared toward minorities.

Generations ago, disabilities on campus were associated with wheelchairs and canes. Today, the definition has been widely expanded. Disabilities can be psychological impairments, mental illness, medical conditions, and many other issues. Because life as a graduate student encompasses many academic skills, students with disabilities sometimes are afraid to even apply. They should be aware that most major universities and colleges now provide campus-wide disability centers that offer confidential discussion about accommodations, as well as providing many other forms of guidance.

The idea of applying to graduate school can be frightening for anyone, but consider if you have disabilities, an entirely new line of questioning comes up. Should you mention this in your personal statement? Should you address a visible disability during an interview? Many other questions also are viewed from a different perspective by students with disabilities.

At the same time, these students have some special resources. An excellent source for researching whether a graduate school meets your needs is AHEAD (**www. ahead.org**), which offers an "Assessment of Campus Climate to Enhance Student Success (ACCESS)." The program provides information on what colleges and graduate schools are doing to help ensure the success of students with disabilities. Typical data covers not only students with disabilities, but also those from diverse backgrounds. This information includes enrollment, retention, attribution, and graduation rates. "The underlying assumption is that students with disabilities are more likely to achieve academic success in a welcoming and fully inclusive accessible environment," according to the group's Web site. There is also the George Washington HEATH Resource Center (**www.heath.gwu. edu**), which is an online clearinghouse on postsecondary education for individuals with disabilities. The HEATH Resource Center Clearinghouse has information about support services, policies, procedures, accessing college or university campuses, career-technical schools, and more The site also has information on financial assistance, scholarships, and other areas.

When it comes to mentioning your disability, there are various reassuring strategies. The decision of whether or not to disclose is a difficult and personal one. You have pride in your accomplishments; at the same time, you may not want to run the risk of rejection because of your disability. This is a legitimate concern. Unless it affects your performance in undergraduate school, it is often a good idea to simply leave it out during your initial application. If it does come up during subsequent interviews, you will have to discuss it. This should be done candidly and objectively. It is not a good idea to do as some students do when confronted with their disability: they assert their Americans with Disabilities Act rights not to answer questions. If you are asked, you should be honest, but add that your disability allows you to function as well as other students. You also do not want to simply ignore the disability. Do not dwell on it, experts say, but shape or present your disability in such a way that it is an advantage. How has it affected your life in positive ways?

One of the first questions you must deal with is whether to attend a graduate school close to home or a university some distance away. Each student will have to make this determination based on their disability and personal preferences.

Regional differences can have a profound impact on students with disabilities because graduate students often find the Northeast and Midwest often have more programs available than the southern and western states. Mass transit is also more accessible in the Midwest and the East. On the other hand, colleges in cold climates may reduce easy access for the disabled.

Physical access is an important issue for the disabled. Is a campus hilly or flat? Are buildings accessible if you are in a wheelchair or have other disabilities? Since the library is a key part of your graduate career, is it easily negotiated? Some schools require graduate students to teach or be research assistants. You need to know if there are facilities accessible to disabled students.

As is the case with all students, disabled candidates are evaluated largely by their performance in undergraduate courses. If your performance as an undergraduate was impacted by a learning disability, for example, you might be able to use other aspects of your candidate profile, such as personal statements and reference letters, to compensate.

You have read one often-repeated suggestion in this book — apply early. This particularly applies to disabled students because they might be in a position where they have to arrange for accommodations and help in coping with their disability during graduate school.

How to Successfully Conduct Informative On-Site Campus Visits

In determining what schools are right for you, much can be learned from reading the catalogs. Read them carefully for information on course selection and faculty, but this information only goes so far. If at all possible, undertake an *informative* visit to the campus. What do we mean by an *informative* visit? Anyone can walk around an Ivy League campus and sit on a bench under tall oak trees. What you need to do is dig beneath the serene surface to determine if this is the *right* place for you.

Why is it important to visit? The simple answer is that it is virtually impossible to get a feel for the school's personality without seeing it for yourself. Every school presents itself as the ideal institution, but only by seeing the campus and visiting with people is it possible to find out if it is really *ideal* for you. You will find all graduate schools welcome your visit. Why not? Your appearance allows them to assess you to help determine whether you will be an asset as a graduate student. Personal visits give you the opportunity to meet with students and faculty. You can observe how students live in an actual, real-life environment. You can observe whether or not you would be able to achieve your own goals and prosper academically there. Your personal visit is important for another reason: When you personally take a look at a school, you are showing that you are a serious person with well-thought-out goals and ambitions.

During a personal visit, you want to determine your comfort level and see what the working and social environment is like. For many students, the beginning of graduate school marks the first time they are away from home towns, families, and friends. It makes sense that you will adjust the fastest and with the least discomfort in a place where you feel comfortable. The more suited your new environment is to your background, the easier the transition will become. For all these reasons, a firsthand look is vital.

It is a good idea to make three visits to any institutions on your short list. Go before you apply, after you have applied, and after you have been accepted. If you are worried about the expense of visiting, the college or university may help you with travel expenses if you are a promising applicant. They are accustomed to such requests. Before you visit, make appointments with the faculty members (who may be out of town when you come, or unavailable for other reasons), admissions officials, and anyone else you might want to see such as financial-aid officers and admissions people. Be sure to also make a date with a graduate advisor.

Many colleges now have virtual tours, which you will certainly want to take a look at before visiting in person. Before your visit, prepare yourself with a list of topics and questions you want to raise. You will make a better impression if you leave out questions that are answered in information sent out to you. Keep in mind that while you are evaluating them, they are also evaluating you. Obviously, you want to make the best impression. You might want to dress somewhat professionally. Be prepared by having specific questions. It is perfectly acceptable to have your questions in a notebook that you produce during interviews. Having questions makes you seem prepared and thoughtful and creates a good impression.

Activity Ideas for Your Campus Visit

- Spend as much time as possible with members of the college community, including professors, and members of extracurricular organizations. Faculty members will want to give you a good impression, but they are not professional recruiters. This is a good time and place to ask them about your prospects for being accepted into programs. Questions to consider at this time include: Does the faculty seem friendly? Are they accessible? Will they help you if you have problems? Keep in mind that few individuals are going to be critical about their programs.

Things to look for include a lack of enthusiasm or vague or general answers to your questions.

- Spend time looking at where students live. Check out prices and areas where you might want to live. Are they acceptable? Consult the free newspapers and brochures available in most areas that advertise homes and apartments.

- Visit the school's financial-aid people. How can they help? Be prepared beforehand to talk about your financial conditions. A face-to-face meeting on this critical matter is highly recommended.

- See the admissions officers. Your goals are to tell the college officials about yourself and find out as much as you can about the college or university. Be prepared to tell the admissions officer about your personal goals, aspirations, and achievements.

- Visit the graduate program director. Ideally, let him or her know of your interest a few weeks beforehand. at which time you can make an appointment.

- Make appointments with other graduate students, if at all possible. If that is not possible, wander around campus and select students at random to question about their experiences. Ask them questions that delve into whether or not they find their programs worthwhile, as well as if they enjoy the overall campus and its general environment. You might find that students love their programs, but dislike living in that particular city. This will help you later when you are serious about determining whether to accept or reject an offer. Graduate students are far more likely to give candid assessments than professors, so consider giving more weight to the opinions of your peers.

- Contact graduate students through their various departments. When you introduce yourself to graduate students as a potential student, they are often happy to talk with you. Do not judge an entire campus by one or two students. Talk to a dozen or so to get a variety of opinions so you can sort them out later.

- Take in the physical nature of the campus. Look carefully at its offices, libraries, laboratories, and other facilities. Read the bulletin boards around campus; they are often good sources of information about a variety of topics.

- Take a walk around town to see areas around the campus. Take a look at what is available in housing and even shopping. Is the shopping convenient, for example, or do you have to drive 45 minutes to find a grocery store? As a graduate student, you will not have a lot of free time and you want basic necessary services to be convenient and nearby.

- Pick a normal school day when there is a regular flow of students on the campus. A weekday is best, but if you have to visit on a Saturday, make sure there will be staff members available to give you a tour, and that you will have access to university buildings. Avoid chaos-filled days such as graduation day.

- Be aware that some colleges and universities have visitation programs, or research programs, that offer an opportunity to take a closer look at the day-to-day operations of the institution. At MIT, for example, departments take advantage of MIT's Spring Weekend in April to encourage prospective students to visit.

- Schedule your visit while the school is in session to get a better idea of the environment when students are around.

- Observe what is offered to assist students' with special needs. You will want to take this into account when looking at all aspects of the school you are evaluating.

- Stay overnight, if possible. It will give you a better feel and add to your understanding of the university as a total entity.

- Sit in on some classes. How do you feel about the size of the classes, the instructors, and the level of competition?

- Read the school newspaper and the local newspaper to get a feel for the area. Look at other sources such as the Internet and local histories that give you clues on local culture and lifestyle.

- Schedule rest time between visits if you are going to more than one school. You want to be mentally fresh to get an accurate impression of each campus.

- Collect the addresses of everyone you meet to later send them gracious thank-you notes. It is not only good manners, but might help you later when you need recommendations or other help.

Briefly

Noted

In many laboratory sciences such as chemistry, new graduate students are often assigned to a potential thesis advisor at the time they enter the school or soon after. This is a critical area because it can be hard to change advisors. Interviewing graduate students about their own advisors is yet another good reason for making personal campus visits.

The Importance of a Good Résumé

You probably do not need to be told the importance of an excellent résumé. Why is a résumé so important? When competing with hundreds or even thousands of other applicants for limited seats in graduate schools, it become essential that your résumé quickly conveys what you can bring to the program in academic abilities, special talents, and real-world experiences. Your résumé can cite the hands-on experience you have had working in independent studies, completing an honors thesis, or working as a research assistant. In addition, your résumé is a chance, in your overall application, to communicate your potential by citing some of the experiences you have already had that are applicable to graduate school.

What you may not know is that there are differences between a CV and a résumé. One of the biggest differences is the audience. The CV is largely geared towards an academic audience. It is a record of your academic and intellectual accomplishments. In contrast, a résumé is read by someone considering hiring you or playing a part in influencing someone's decision to accept or reject your admission to graduate school. Think of a CV as a compelling introduction to your experiences and skills as they relate to graduate school. A CV almost invariably displays your academic credentials and accomplishments in more detail than a résumé does.

Should You Use a Résumé or a CV for Admission to Graduate School?

If you are applying to a college or a university for a degree program, or to a law, business, or medical school, a résumé is generally preferable.

If you are applying for a medical fellowship and have numerous publications, presentations, and abstract submissions, the preferred format is the CV. CVs, unlike résumés, may be longer than one or two pages in length, and often exceed ten pages when the candidate has numerous publication credits.

The general order of a résumé is as follows: an opening summary that provides an admission director with a "snapshot" of you as a candidate. This section also lists your most relevant accomplishments, such as perfect test scores or being class valedictorian.

This section is followed by your education: where you went to school, and notable achievements such as making the Dean's List or other academic accomplishments.

The third section is generally volunteer work. It is preferable to list work that coincides with your future goals. If you are planning to study psychology, for example, you might list the time you spent working in a homeless or battered women's shelter.

The fourth section lists your hobbies and other interests. It is preferable here also to list those activities that coincide with your future goals. If you are looking at a fashion career, for example, you can say here that you have been working with fabrics and sewing at home.

What is a simple résumé? It is an overview of your education, experiences, skills, and other relevant information. It should be a candid, self-promotional document that presents you in the best possible light. There is no strict set format for a résumé, but there are general guidelines.

There are many different opinions about the best way to write a résumé. Realistically, you should keep in mind there is no single "best way." Writing a résumé is an art, not an exact science.

When writing your résumé, you should pay careful attention to two elements: visual appeal and relevance. Both are important.

There are several types of résumés and which one you choose depends largely on your experience. The most popular one is chronological. It lists your experiences in reverse chronological order. This type of résumé is best for someone who wants to emphasize job or work experience, or someone who has been employed for a few years and is now looking to attend graduate school.

The best choice of résumé for a newly graduated college student trying to get into a graduate school is the modified chronological résumé. In this format, your experiences are grouped by their function. Instead of bringing out your work background, this format can emphasize your leadership experience, technical background, and other advantages you can cite that are not work related.

Some students prefer functional résumés that group their various experiences by the skills they have used. Those skills might involve leadership, organizational ability, or volunteer programs.

Another type of résumé is a combination of chronological and functional that lists your experiences chronologically, while classifying the descriptions used within your experiences by your particular skills. These skills might include leadership abilities or analytical or communication areas where you have excelled.

The following is a sample résumé of a young college graduate applying to graduate school.

Sample Résumé
Sally Jones

Campus:	Permanent:
ABC College Street	XYZ Home Street
Gainesville, FL 32608	Ocala, FL 34472
301-235-8576	301-246-7589
SallyJ@internet.com	SallyJ@internet.com

Objective

Complete graduate school in the field of education and teach at the college level

Sample Résumé

Summary

Teacher certification for Secondary Education

Cum Laude graduate with B.A. degree

Completed Student Teaching in Private School System

Education

Bachelor or Arts in English with a minor in Education

University of Florida, Gainesville, FL

Graduated Cum Laude with 3.6 GPA

Courses taken included Grammar (Honors Class), Psychology, Educational Technology, Classroom Management, Parent and Teacher Relations

Experience

Student Teaching, August 2007 to February, 2008

Ocala Private School System, Florida

Accomplishments

- Co-taught English classes for Grade 11

- Served as Teacher Assistant for Grades 10 and 11

- Awarded "Student Teacher of the Year Award"

Volunteer Work

- Co-Headed a local literacy campaign in conjunction with the public library

- Assisted with planning educational field trips to watch plays to enhance learning about dramatic arts

Sample Résumé
Other Activities
Student Exchange Program, College of London, England
Dorm Resident Assistant at Broward Hall, University of Florida

The sample résumé is simple and down-to-earth. It deals in facts about this student. It lists the student's school and work background as well as awards and outstanding features of this would-be graduate candidate. In this case, the student had a high GPA so she chose to include it. Obviously, if your own GPA is not high, you would not put it on your résumé. This student also pointed out her various awards and activities outside of class. Admissions committee members like to see well-rounded students who do more than compile high GPAs. The format is also attractive because, while it is not elaborate or fancy, it is positioned in such a way that it is appealing to the eyes of an admissions committee member who wants to do a quick scan of this student's background.

Whatever type of résumé you choose, there are certain mandatory sections. These include:

- **Contact information.** You must include your name, address, telephone number, and e-mail address at the top of a résumé. Some students make the mistake of using an informal e-mail address they have used in college such as joeblow@superstud43. If you have such an e-mail address, change it immediately to something that sounds more professional.

- **Education.** This section should immediately follow your contact information. If you have several years of work experience, consider placing this section farther down on your résumé. Include where you went to school and the dates you attended.

- **Experience.** If you are going right from college to graduate school, you will have limited experience, but you can include your volunteer efforts such as working with the elderly, or part-time jobs that also contributed to your education, such as working as an assistant to some of your college teachers. Perhaps you have published articles somewhere. Be sure to include that type of information.

- **GPAs.** The question often comes up of whether or not to include your GPA on your résumé. If your GPA is high and you are magna/summa cum laude, you will certainly want to include it. If your GPA is not outstanding, leave it out. There is no rule that it must be included.

CASE STUDY: ALBERT EINSTEIN

Albert Einstein, one of the most brilliant men of modern times, would have had a difficult time getting into graduate school today. He had what is described as a "bumpy ride" through high school and college. He did not have high grades. As a young man, the noted scientist had a lot of trouble finding a job to support himself and his wife.

CASE STUDY: ALBERT EINSTEIN

A friend managed to get him work in a patent office in Bern. Switzerland. While there, Einstein became a technical expert in evaluating patent proposals. He became proficient in finding flaws in designs and in deciding whether gadgets would actually work. In his free time, he wrote and published scientific papers on various areas of physics. If Einstein were alive today and applying to graduate school in science, he would be advised not to mention his scholastic record, but he would certainly want to point out his accomplishments as a technical expert, and cite the papers he published as evidence of his ability to do good work as a student in the future.

List relevant tasks in concise, bulleted points. Avoid long phrases and blocks of text that are difficult to read. Consider what is relevant to the person who is reading your résumé.

Years ago, tradition had it that everyone had to have an "objective." That is no longer the case, though it is an option if you want to include more information on your résumé. The question of references also comes up frequently. They are generally unnecessary. If you choose to include them, you can put them on a separate piece of paper.

Should you include an opening summary, or a summary listing your goals or qualifications? These have become increasingly common in today's résumé world, but they are optional in your case. Some schools frown on them. It is best to find out the policy of the university where you are applying.

Some students think that everything they have ever done

should be put on their résumé. This is counter-productive. You can safely skip that odd job you had as a "sandwich artist" at a sub shop, for example. Leave out any skills that are irrelevant to attending graduate school. It should not be too difficult to determine what you can leave out.

The issue of self-promotion often comes up with résumés. Some students object to the notion because it is so obviously self-serving. But promoting yourself does not mean you have to exaggerate or "hype" your past accomplishments. You are merely emphasizing your most noteworthy attainments, while down playing your failures, assuming you have some. You want to be honest and point out specific accomplishments, providing precise details whenever possible. This makes your accomplishments much more believable.

You may have heard that the average résumé gets about 15 seconds of attention. You have a short time to get someone's attention, which makes it crucial for your résumé to be well organized and easy to read. Most documents are scanned from top to bottom and from left to right. That makes design also a factor. You do not want an "artistic" résumé with a lot of fancy swirls and elaborate type, but you do want to convey some visual appeal. You can select and organize the material you want to present with little or no help, but when it comes to the design of your résumé, you might want to consult with friends or get professional help.

How long should an ideal résumé be? Try one page. Hardly anyone will even look at a second or third page. Condense all information into a one-page format that presents your case for graduate school in the best possible light.

Now that you have gathered all the necessary materials for your résumé, how do you evaluate it? Here are a dozen considerations to help you decide if you are on the right track:

1. Did you use the full name of the college where you are applying? Students often unthinkingly shorten names.

2. Did you use large enough type? Not all fonts are alike, and very small ones discourage readers who do not have the hawk-like eyes of younger students. For example Times New Roman, which is a popular type, is smaller than Verdana. Choose at least 10-point type.

3. Did you use overly wordy descriptions in your objective and elsewhere. Check whether you were succinct in your sentences. You do not have to write in complete sentences in a résumé.

4. Check for typos. These are common and make you look bad. The reader may think that, if you made mistakes in your résumé, you might be careless about typos when you are a graduate student.

5. Your tone should be simple and clear. Check to see that you have maintained that tone throughout your résumé.

6. Did you get too fancy in your layout and design? Unless you are applying to art school, you want to keep it straight and simple.

7. Did you avoid stretching your experiences or exaggerating your importance?

8. Is your format consistent throughout the résumé? Pay attention to spacing; white space; and use of bullets, headings, and any features you highlighted in any way.

9. Did you use action words and avoid repeating any single word? Many résumé writers use a phrase or term, such as "multitasked," far too often.

10. Did you include all your contact information such as name, address, e-mail, and more?

11. Did you include some courses that might be relevant to your graduate field? This helps demonstrate your interest and helps add to your being viewed as a serious candidate for graduate school.

12. Did you include specific skills such as computer skills, languages, technical skills, or lab experiences?

Since it is impossible to be objective when it comes to your own life, it is always a good move to have a friend or colleague review your résumé. He or she can help you determine how others will view your accomplishments. Do not just settle for someone saying "it is good." Get some details. Ask your reviewer questions. You may have to re-write your résumé several times to get it right.

When it comes to a résumé, what is often important is what you leave out. For example, you left out your minor jobs as a paperboy and working as a clerk in a health food store. But perhaps you included phrases such as, "References furnished upon request." That is not necessary because it is viewed as a common assumption. Personal information such as age, marital, or health status, and even race and ethnicity should also be omitted.

White space is important. Do not try to cram everything in your résumé. Open it up and give it a generous amount of air. It will make your résumé more likely to be read and absorbed. If you do not believe that, look at the advertisements you read in a newspaper. The best-read ads have a lot of white space. It is simply good communication.

Going Beyond the Obvious:
A Few Extra Things to Help Ensure Success

Did you know that on a state level, a higher proportion of students are generally admitted from the school's home state than other areas? That obviously gives you an advantage if you are living in a state with an Ivy League or top university.

Your chances of being accepted also increase when you can describe an array of talents. Graduate admissions offices are trying to sort through many qualified candidates, and it is easier to narrow down the successful candidates if they can identify the ones who have a diverse variety of talents. Admissions officers see these candidates as clearly standing out. It is in your best interest to demonstrate or show off all the various abilities you possess.

What other "extras" should you know to help you get accepted to graduate school?

In many ways, knowledge is as powerful a tool here as in the rest of life. Knowing how to find graduate programs, for example, is something you might not have considered. But thorough and painstaking research in this area might turn up a top school that seems perfect for your particular background. You cannot get into a graduate program you did not know existed.

In the ideal world, you will have taken the following steps before you applied to graduate school:

- You strived for a high GPA. A 3.6 GPA and above is recommended for the most competitive schools.

- You started the application process early. You

realized that this will give you a leg up on much of your competition for acceptance, and will also allow you to do things thoroughly and in order.

- You researched what test or tests you will be required to take in order to apply. You invested in some study guides or other materials and spent some serious time tackling the practice tests. You are smart enough that you would not even think about taking the LSAT, MCAT, GRE, or other test without a good test guide, and without spending hours and hours studying it. Many people who apply to grad school do not think it is worth the time or money to buy a study guide and use it. They are wrong, so you have an advantage over them.

- You took as many advanced courses as possible in your field. You got to know your professors. You engaged them and let them know of your interest in going on to grad school. You tried to find ways to be of assistance to them in their teaching or research.

- You carefully reviewed all materials available from colleges you were considering.

- You strengthened your language skills. Many arts and humanities graduate programs have considerable language requirements.

- You successfully sought out some research experience. You did this in your junior year or you participated in a senior thesis program.

- You continued always to improve your writing skills. You are aware that your ability to write well is crucial both for admission and your ultimate success in your particular field.

- You studied and prepared for specific application requirements. For example, you found out you needed to develop a portfolio of artwork or recording of musical compositions to submit as part of the graduate school application.

If you have completed all these things, you also need to be sure you have *accurately* portrayed your activities and experiences. Hopefully, you did this in detail.

To practice for tests, buy books, use tutors, take a class, or hire a consulting service. These are all ways that students "ace" tests. When taking tests, you should always strive to do your best the first time, but realize you can take tests repeatedly. While some schools will use your highest scores, others will take an average. There is no set procedure.

If done properly, the application essay (or personal statement) is a chance for you to make yourself stand apart from other applicants. Some admissions counselors make initial judgments about an application's strengths and standing by grading the personal statement before any other part of the application.

Of course, you cannot go back and change your grades, class rank, or standardized test scores, but you can control the quality of your application essay. You can use key tools of writing and rewriting and editing to produce a gleaming document.

Your application essay should show self-awareness, honesty, and depth. Avoid ego-driven autobiographies, lying, or exaggerating about circumstances. At the same time, be certain your essay is free of typos and misspellings.

Admission officers often give high priority to strong letters of recommendation. Persuasive writing can turn the heads of admissions committees, while average letters will almost certainly reduce a student's chances of being accepted. It is important to be careful when selecting the two or three people you want to write your letters. Get people who know you and your potential.

View your personal statement and application essays as comparable to marketing material. The analogy is a good one. Indeed, many admissions books talk about "Marketing Yourself to... " Here are three key suggestions in this area: (1) Do not make broad claims of desirable attributes; let the reader experience those attributes through your activities. (2) Learn from the admissions committees. They are telling you what they want to know in their questions; answer them directly and read their brochures and other material. (3) Let your personal statement embody the qualities you are trying to convey; try to write like a professional, even if you are not one.

From an admissions office standpoint, here are other tips that will help you go beyond the standard requirements:

- Admissions officers are looking for strong GPAs from their candidates, but they are also looking at your special experiences. You can gain such experiences through academic internships, summer jobs, and off-campus study programs.

- Admissions committees also look closely at your statement of purpose. It has been described as an intellectual résumé and is one of the most — if not *the* most — important component of your application. Faculty members look for intellectual vitality and promise. They want to learn the highlights of your academic preparation for their program. They also want to know about your research and creative future interests, and why the school is a good fit for you.

- You also should know that admissions officers often give more credit to grades in traditional college classes than easier classes.

- Admissions officers like to see applicants who have shown leadership in one or more volunteer or extracurricular activities. Quality is better than quantity. Joining a dozen clubs is not as effective as showing a deep and long-term leadership role in at least one club.

- Graduate school officers want to see both passion and commitment to your field of study. Some of the best programs require you to have experience in your field. For example, some of the best MBA programs do not admit applicants who do not have several years of related work experience. Similarly, the best law schools and medical schools want to see that you have had exposure in these respective professions.

- Describing your early exposure to a field can offer effective insight into your core objectives. Be careful not to make your points cliché-ridden. For example, do not start an essay by saying "I have always wanted to be . . . " Instead, include specific content in your essay.

- Graduate school is a means to an end, and admissions committees prefer students who know where they are going and to what use they will put their education. The occasional soul-searcher who exhibits exceptional raw potential is also welcomed.

Here are a dozen tips to improve your chances of being accepted:

1. Start your planning for graduate school as early as possible. Taking tests, researching schools, getting applications sent off in a timely fashion, and the various writing duties you have to

complete takes a lot of time. If you wait until the last minute, you will be rushed and stressed. It will be difficult to give it your best effort.

2. Apply to more than one school. Some people apply to 20 or more, but two or three is a more manageable number. It is simple common sense not to put all your hopes in one school.

3. The admissions process for graduate schools is nothing like the process that undergraduate colleges and universities use. There, decisions are made by the admissions department. For grad school, the professors in the department make the decisions. It is a much more personal choice.

4. When you are visiting schools, talk to the professors there. Let them know how much you want to work with them. Try to convey what a good student you are, and how you would be an outstanding asset to their program. Talk to them about you and your goals with enthusiasm and passion, and do not grovel.

5. Get a sky-high score on the Graduate Record Exam or Graduate Management Admission Test. Overall, GRE and GMAT scores range from 200 to 800; strive for 700 and above. This is easier said than done, but it will be a tremendous help if you can get a high score.

6. If you have written any articles for publication, be sure to include a copy of them in your application package. Since writing and researching is what grad school is all about, you will be demonstrating that you can do the work. It also helps that your writing was good enough for publication.

7. Keep up with new developments in the departments of any universities you hope to attend. If you learn that one college recently received a large grant for research purposes, or was given a large gift by a donor, that could mean they will be looking to accept more than the usual number of new graduate students because of their higher budget.

8. Do not rush to submit your application in the first round. Different schools operate on different schedules but in general, B-schools accept one round of applications and another in February. There is no reason to rush.

9. Be prepared to discuss any weak spots in your résumé or your undergraduate transcript. Do not just ignore poor grades in one semester. Instead, explain that perhaps you were ill with mononucleosis and your grades suffered. Turn this around into a positive about how you rebounded from an illness and significantly raised your grades the next semester.

10. Have others review your application. They may find flaws, errors or omissions. You do not need a lot of people, but do try to find at least one or two others to give their evaluation.

11. If you are put on the "wait list," do not give up. Instead, make the most of it. Students often assume being put on the wait list is the same as being rejected but that is wrong. There are remedies here as well. Say your test stores were low. You can take the tests again and hopefully have a higher score. You can then apply again with new information about your acceptability. You also will want to keep in touch with the admissions committee. This does not mean daily briefings, but it is perfectly acceptable to send a letter if you have new developments in your life such as higher test scores.

12. If you are like many students, and not sure if you want to earn a master's or a doctorate, think about applying for the doctoral program. Most professors and departments give strong preference to doctoral candidates over students studying for their master's. This could be a deciding factor in your being accepted.

One final suggestion: be yourself. Students often have an image in their minds of the type of student the top schools want to recruit. The reality is that graduate school admissions committees aim to enroll a broad mix of different personalities and widely varied backgrounds.

For that reason alone, the committees want to know a lot about your background. So do not be evasive. Tell them the truth. Let them get to know the real you.

Have You Forgotten Anything?

It is sometimes said the best mistakes are the ones we learn from. But in your graduate school application process, you would rather get it right the first time. If you have a tendency to be forgetful, double check and triple check to make sure you have not forgotten anything. Even if you are normally not forgetful, it is always a good idea to create a checklist and do a final review to see that you have included all the required elements of your application.

Some universities have a student-managed application process in which the student is responsible for collecting all the letters of reference, transcripts, and other material, and ensuring all of it gets to the university by the deadline. Other schools use a system where bits and pieces of the application come in over a period of time. Obviously it is more convenient for evaluators if all the material comes in one package. Check to see what system the various universities use. Online applications allow you to submit the application form and application fee via your computer. All other documentation still has to be sent in by mail. You will need to check out the particular systems used by the schools of your choice.

Most schools will advise you on what is missing, but

do not count on them to catch all your errors. You are ultimately responsible for ensuring all missing material is supplied prior to the final deadline for completed applications.

If you wonder how you can find out more about the various applications (and general information as well) at the different universities, here are six sources of information:

1. *Peterson's Guide* is among the best-known places to find comprehensive information about graduate schools. *The Gourman Report* and *U.S. News & World Report's Graduate School Issue* also rate the schools. If you have a particular major you are looking at such as architecture or archeology, there are various guides. Archeological students, for example, can find the AAA Guide to Departments, which lists nearly all programs around the world. This guide is very useful because its department listings include faculty, research interests, special programs, brief descriptions of program requirements, funding available, and so on.

2. University libraries have calendars from just about every university. Graduate facilities may also have copies of calendars you can consult.

3. Most departments have Web pages that give you full information on their graduate programs such

as faculty, research interests, and more. You can often submit a request for an application through a link on the Web page.

4. Talk to faculty members in your particular field about possible schools. All of them have been through a graduate program. They all have contacts at other schools and are generally familiar with at least some other program procedures and requirements.

5. You can write the school and ask them to send you information on their programs and background information on what you need to know when applying.

6. Both departments and faculty offices will have notice boards displaying flyers and posters that advertise graduate programs.

Since writing is an important part of your graduate school application, check to be sure that everything you have done is first-rate. Remember that your primary reading audience is admissions officials who want to know the following information:

- Why do you want to do graduate study? What are your academic interests?

- Why is the department in question a good department for you? Why are you a good candidate for that particular department?

- Are there particular faculty members in the department who you are interested in working with? If so, do not be afraid to name them. Doing so is a good way of showing that you have thoroughly researched the faculty interests, and have given thought to your suitability for that particular department. Leave extensive flattery out of your opinions.

- How does studying in this department fit in with your long-term plans? How is it a continuation of what you have learned as an undergraduate?

When writing their personal statement, many students try to use a one-piece-fits-all approach, but that should not be done in the graduate application process. Personalize your statement for each graduate school, or write separate ones. The personal statement is a communication between you and *this particular* graduate school. The admissions committee wants to feel like you are talking to them. If you have done your research on the departments you are applying to, you should be able to judge the changes you need to make to your personal statement when applying to different schools.

Hopefully, you also remembered that this is not a time for clichés. You have not said something like "I am hard-working, serious, and enthusiastic about engineering." You should have done some thinking on this and only written sentences with substantive content.

A straightforward and informative personal statement that steers clear of platitudes speaks volumes about your commitment and academic personality. Everyone wants to convey that they are enthusiastic, committed, and able. You should be the one who stands out from the crowd by communicating these things without actually saying them.

The entire application process is so complicated that it is easy to miss something. It is a good idea to contact faculty members or other representatives of your particular department. Depending on the department, you might find that you have established e-mail correspondence with some people before even sending away your application.

If you correspond with a faculty member, it is not a good idea to get overly informal or chatty. Be friendly, but do not address them using their first name even if they sign their e-mails with it. It is safer to stick with "Dear Professor X."

Check to make sure that you did not send anything the application instructions did not ask for. Do not send your CV if it is not asked for, for example. Some schools do want to see all applicants' CVs, but to send something unwanted is courting disaster because admissions officials are busy enough without the added weight of correspondence they have no interest in seeing.

Hopefully, you also remembered to ask for academic transcripts from all of your current or former higher-education institutions well in advance. Usually they reach you in two to three weeks. Also, ask for plenty of copies. Many graduate schools want you to send two or even three copies with your application.

All applications may look the same, but check that you read the directions carefully. Application forms can vary.

Here are some common stumbling blocks:

- Your letters of recommendation never were sent out. You asked that the letters be sent directly to the university, but busy professors procrastinated. If your requested letters are being sent directly to the university, you may have to remind your letter-writers in a gentle fashion if there are any delays.

- Compute your GPA according to the instructions. Different schools use different methods.

- Be careful not to confuse "country" with "county." That is a very common but easily avoidable error.

- Do not forget to sign your application or recommendation letter waivers.

- Be sure to list your intended major. If you are not sure, write "undecided."

- When a college asks for senior year classes, be

sure to submit your classes for the entire year, not just the first semester.

- Include a permanent address. The address you use should be one that the college can contact you at any time in the admissions process.

- If you are asked what grade level you are entering, write down the level for the next academic year.

- When you are asked to list your activities, do not limit yourself to activities in college. Include work with community organizations, volunteer efforts, and part-time or full-time work.

- For "nickname," include your preferred name, if you have one (Jim, instead of James). Do not write in the names your friends use when they joke around with you — avoid "Squid" or "Buster."

- If the application asks for "zip code + 4," enter your entire nine-digit zip code. If you are not sure what your nine-digit zip code is, consult the U.S. Postal Service. Do not get this wrong or your mail could be delayed.

- It always helps to have others look over all your application forms. Sometimes, it is the little things that hurt your chances for admission.

- Use the spell checker on all your papers, but keep in mind it is not infallible. For example, this statement, "I no a lot about applying two college" would get by the spell checker. Proofread and get someone to help, if at all possible.

- Double check the spelling of the name of the school where you are applying.

- Watch out for errors in entering dates. A frequent error is that students list the current year instead of their birth year (for example, they write they were born 1/1/06, instead of 1/1/86).

- If you are going to use some of your responses for more than one school, be sure to replace the name of the school with the correct one, For instance, while doing an application for Princeton, you do not want to say "this is why I want to go to Brown."

Complete a draft copy of your application before you start working on the final draft. That way, you will avoid some of these mistakes.

Your best chances for submitting a great application package is to allow a lot of time to complete it. That will keep you from making many of the errors you might have overlooked. This way, you will not have to learn from your mistakes. Instead, you avoided them entirely.

CHAPTER 6

You Are In...
What Now?

Paying for Your Degree

Now that you have been accepted, what is your next area of concern? That is an easy question. The answer is more complicated.

You are going to have to pay tuition and related expenses such as books. You also need enough money to live. Graduate school generally costs more than undergraduate. There is no doubt that graduate school is expensive, costing anywhere from $20,000 a year to $50,000 or more at a law school. Non-professional graduate degrees do not cost as much as law and medical degrees, but they are still expensive.

Tuition is the first cost you think of when considering graduate school. But there is another major price tag as well: the loss of income while you are in school. The good news is that, even if you do not have wealthy parents or a spouse who makes a good living, there are various sources you can tap to pay for your new life as a graduate student.

If you are like most graduate students, you will need a combination of your own money, earned income, loans, and perhaps other sources of money. You will not be relying on a single source of finances, but on a variety of sources.

Take a serious look at your financial condition. If you have a spouse who works and earns enough for the two of you to live on, your life will be easier. Even if a spouse earns enough money for everyday living expenses, you will still have to consider tuition, books, and other costs of going to graduate school.

First have to figure out your fixed costs. That is fairly easy when you add up tuition, books, and other costs of school.

At this stage, if you do not have a lot of money in the bank, consider changing your lifestyle. Perhaps you have some luxury products that you no longer use like a jet ski or a boat. Perhaps you have a luxury automobile. If you are going to an urban school where there is mass transit, you might want to sell your car and opt for a bicycle or plan on walking to class. Perhaps you can change your lifestyle to cut back on spending. Maybe you treated yourself at the end of the week to a $40 meal at an expensive restaurant. You might cut back that luxury and save yourself more than $600 a semester. You could also consider eliminating that $3 cup of coffee at Starbucks, buying a coffee pot and bringing a thermos to school. There are a lot of lifestyle changes that can save you money in graduate school.

Briefly

Noted

"A penny saved is a penny earned."

Ben Franklin

Calculate the cost of living in the area where you are going to school. Columbia University is one of the top schools, but because it is in New York City, it also carries one of the highest cost of living rates in the world. You can find comparisons of the cost of living at sites such as **www.runheimzer.com**. There are also sites that will compare the area where you live now with where you want to attend graduate school such as **www.cnnmoney.com** and **www.salary.com**.

There are many other factors to consider .Does your spouse has a job; will he or she be able to find one at your new school? If you have a family, will your college provide insurance, or will you have to factor that into your cost-of-living budget as well?

After figuring out your fixed costs of being a student, you will need to work out a budget of what it will cost you to live for two years or more. Here are some essentials of planning for school-related costs:

- Tuition. There are usually huge differences in cost for state residents versus out-of-state students

- Fees

- Health insurance, which may or may not be included in the fees

- Books

- Travel and local transportation such as parking and auto insurance

- Computers, art supplies, or other items necessary for your particular program

Briefly noted: *Consult with your school's financial aid office for advice on all aspects of your financial situation.*

You will need a separate budget for your everyday life. Housing will almost certainly be your biggest expense. That will cost you several hundred dollars a month or more. You can save money on housing by making arrangements as early as possible after you have been accepted. At most schools, as time goes by, there are fewer choices. This is particularly true if you are looking at student housing.

The second biggest part of your domestic budget will be groceries. How much do you spend a week or a month at the food store? If you are looking at a tight budget, think about where you can cut back — desserts, for example, or expensive imported beer. There are also many mundane things you probably take for granted such as laundry costs. There is also the matter of lifestyle. You will spend a lot of time working in graduate school, but you do not want to live like a monk. You might want to keep your cable TV, for example, or your long-distance telephone service. Many of these minor decisions depend on you and your lifestyle and how you can afford to maintain it. If you can get by without a car, you will save hundreds and perhaps thousands of dollars a year.

There are three main sources of funds for graduate school. The first and best is your own money. It is best to pay as much as you can and not go heavily into debt. Some graduate students try to work full-time and go to school. This seldom works well. Given the choice, part-time work is better. Other students take part-time jobs and sometimes find that, because of their expertise, they can make money tutoring school children or even college undergraduates. Many graduate schools have work-study programs. Work for study does not have to be repaid. The work you do is not washing dishes in the school's cafeteria, either. Many students find work-study is academic work directly or indirectly related to their field. They are essentially being paid to further their education and training.

If you are working already and returning to school, you might find that your employer will help pay expenses. This is a growing trend. Something to keep in mind about tuition reimbursement programs is that you will probably have to pay the school yourself up front (something you will have to budget for), and your employer will reimburse you at the end of a semester or quarter. If you are working for an employer willing to help you pay your graduate school costs, you have got one more encouraging reason to return to school.

The second main source of money for graduate students is the federal government through their student-loan programs. Pell Grants, which do not have to be repaid, are available only to undergraduate students. The government's main loan program is the Stafford Federal Loan program. Some of this money comes directly from government and some comes from banks. Stafford Student Loans are not based on financial need, nor is credit approval required. There are two kinds of Stafford Student Loans, subsidized and unsubsidized. With subsidized loans, you will not be charged any interest as long as you remain in school half-time. These loans do not have to be repaid until six months after you leave school. With an unsubsidized loan, you will be charged interest immediately upon graduation. You can borrow up to $18,500 a year with both types of loan, with a cap of $138,500. The federal government also offers Perkins Loans, for which you need to demonstrate financial need to be eligible.

The third major source of financial aid is the graduate school itself. There is a big difference between university- or college-based loans and those coming from the government. One of the biggest differences is that much of the aid to graduate students from the school is handled by individual departments. Faculty members in each department often have discretionary power to allocate aid. You can find out more information from your particular department.

University or college financial aid can take many other forms as well. For example, there are fellowships. These are undoubtedly the most desirable form of aid because they are a gift; no repayment is required.

There is also the assistantship. The two most common are teaching and research assistantships. These programs also provide you with financial help that does not have to be paid back.

Five considerations to look at when evaluating your financial solutions:

1. **Plan ahead.** Get organized. Once you determine your school's overall costs and how much you and your spouse can earn, you will have a much better idea of how much financial help you will need.

2. **Look for free money first.** Start by studying scholarships, grants, fellowships, and paid internships. If you are employed, check with your company about tuition reimbursement. Take advantage of programs that will not cost you now, and that you will not have to pay for in the future.

3. **Determine whether your savings, scholarships, and other options can meet your projected budget.** If that is not the case, look first into government loans. Get started by filling out the free application for Federal Student Aid (FAFSA). Look into other government loans as well.

4. **Research alternative loans.** They may meet the needs you cannot meet through government loans. These are less desirable, however, in part because of higher interest rates.

5. **If necessary, choose a private lender.** You will find these services are everywhere. Choosing a good one is always a challenge, but word of mouth can help you. Check with other students to find out about their experiences with these lenders. Ask questions about who will be servicing your loan and in what time frame How long will the lender take to process your application and disburse funds? Consider combining your loans. If all your loans are of the same type, they can be consolidated into one monthly payment. That can lower your payment and make re-payment easier.

CASE STUDY: STANFORD UNIVERSITY

Stanford University's Financial Aid office put a sample graduate student budget on its Web site. The budget applies to the typical Stanford graduate student who is unmarried and attending full-time for autumn, winter, and spring quarters (AWS). Individual room and board charges, books, supplies, and personal expenses will vary from the standard budget estimate. The cost of education on which loans and work-study are based includes the expense categories listed below as well as tuition charges.

* Tuition charges listed here reflect the School of Humanities and Sciences. Budgets will differ if a student's attendance or enrolled units vary from the standards, says Stanford, or if the student is married or has dependent children.

CASE STUDY: STANDFORD UNIVERSITY Standard Graduate Student Budget 2007-2008 Estimated Cost of Attendance On-Campus			
	Quarterly		**AWS Quarters**
Books and Supplies	$547		$1,641
Rent, Food, Personal	$5,406		$16,218
Transportation	$263		$789
Medical Insurance	$684		$2,052
Total Living Allowance	**$6,900**		**$20,700**
Full-Time Tuition*			
Tuition	$11,600		$34,800
Total Costs	**$18,500**		**$55,500**
Maximum student loans	**$18,500**		**$55,500**
Tuition at 8–10 Unit Rate			
Tuition	$8,040		$24,120
Total Costs	**$14,940**		**$44,820**
Maximum Student Loans	**$14,940**		**$44,820**

Stanford also says that tuition charges for graduate students depend on the school and number of enrolled units. Full-time for many students will be eight to ten units per quarter, while for others it may be in excess of ten units per quarter. The best source of information about typical enrollment patterns for a particular program is the academic department.

So as you can see, a graduate degree is not easy and it is not cheap, but it could well be worth your effort. U.S. Census Bureau studies show that people holding doctoral degrees earned 79.2 percent more, on average, than persons holding only bachelor's degrees. People holding professional degrees earned 118.7 percent more, on average, than persons holding bachelor's degrees.

Average earnings for persons with advanced degrees are even more impressive when it comes to total dollar figures. A person with a bachelor's degree is expected to earn an average of $2.1 million dollars in his or her lifetime, while a person with a master's degree will earn approximately $2.5 million, according to a recent study.

As more people go to college, the bachelor's degree comes closer to what the high school diploma used to be — an entry-level degree. This is particularly true in the fields of science, engineering, and mathematics, where an advanced degree is almost a requirement for a successful career in your chosen field.

You must decide whether graduate school is worth the monetary investment it will require.

Key Elements of Financial Aid

You have figured out how much graduate school is going to cost you. Chances are you will not have enough financial support from your sources to pay for all your schooling. What you need to know now is what are the key elements of financial aid.

The good news is that there are vast amounts of financial aid available. You will almost certainly qualify for some of it. The federal government issues loans, but so do states in some cases.

In some ways, the federal government is generous to graduate students. As we have discussed, the major federal program is Stafford Loans, which do have to be repaid, but are not based on financial need. Perkins Loans, on the other hand, require that you demonstrate financial need to be eligible.

Another type of loan is the Graduate PLUS, which are available to students enrolled at least half-time in a graduate or professional program. These loans are limited and subject to credit reviews, so an applicant with an unfavorable credit history will only be able to obtain the loan with an endorser.

Your first course of action here is to fill out a Free Application for Federal Student Aid (FAFSA), which FAFSA on its Web site says is perhaps the single most important form related to financial aid. The site also provides some tips on correctly filling out the forms to ensure that you are eligible for the maximum amount. Here are some tips to help you through this process:

- You will need IRS tax returns.

- Always check basic elements like addresses and zip codes.

- "Nothing will kill a FAFSA faster than errors or omissions," the site says.

- The form has a "save" button, but not on every page. Be sure you save it if you are filing online.

- Print out the paper version and do a "practice run." If you encounter technical difficulties, you will not lose all your earlier information.

- You will need your Social Security Number, your driver's license number, current bank statements, and other investment information.

Be sure and do this early because these funds are not unlimited. The graduate school of your choice will have these multipage forms on hand. Some universities will require you to fill out their own forms before you can receive financial aid. The idea behind that is a simple one: The fact that money is available does not necessarily mean you want to borrow to the limit. After they graduate, some students report misgivings about having gotten so heavily into debt. You will want to have a realistic idea of how much you are borrowing and what your monthly payments will be. You should also research starting salaries in your field, and see if the pays will be enough to ensure that you can make your loan payments.

The good news is that you will find it is far easier to get loans and other forms of aid than it was as an undergraduate. This is the case because many forms of aid are based on a student's financial need, which in turn, is based on the differences between the cost of going to school and the financial contribution that is expected from the student's family. Undergraduate students are usually declared as dependents, while graduate students have the tendency to be independent, meaning that financial help of some kind is more necessary and more likely to be available.

If you cannot get a large enough loan from the government, you can look at private student loans. There are many of them to choose from, but they should be a last resort because federal loans are almost always preferable. If you have exhausted all options, however, such as federal loans, scholarships, and grants, you might consider the private sector. They can often offer loans of up to $40,000 a year, sometimes more.

Unlike federal loans, a private loan is based on your credit score. Sometimes, you can get a lower rate because you are using the money for education, but do not count on it. Most major financial institutions offer private student loans.

Banking institutions also make it relatively easy to borrow money this way. They have the disadvantage of usually carrying higher interest rates. This is something you should consider in some depth. Graduate students sometimes find that this is their only alternative. If you determine that you need to follow this route to pay for your degree, consider the following factors:

- What is the interest rate? You certainly want the lowest, though you will have to look at other factors.

- Not all banks are unscrupulous, but you want to look carefully at loans with low interest rates that sometimes skyrocket after a few months.

- How much can you borrow? What is the limit?

- What time period does the loan cover? One semester, two semesters, or a year?

- Can your loan be increased if you find later on that you do not have enough money?

- When is the loan due to be paid off? Many institutions make these loans with the stipulation that you do not have to repay until you graduate. Some loans offer a longer grace period such as six months or a year before you have to start paying the money back.

- Does your lender require your loan to be certified by your school? Direct-to-consumer loans often have much higher interest rates than private alternative loans, which require school certification.

- Do you need a co-signer? Are you able to get one? You will often need one if you are a recent college graduate entering graduate school and have not yet established a credit rating.

- If you supply a co-signer, is there a lower interest rate?

- How much are origination fees? These are the amounts paid to the bank for services in originating the loan. The fee can typically range from 1 to 3 percent. Look for lenders (definitely in the minority) who charge no origination or early payment fees.

Student staff offices usually do not recommend lenders, but they will help you find available choices. The quickest way to evaluate loans of this type is online. Most institutions offer all the information you will need on their Web sites. Sometimes, you can apply via telephone. Be fully aware that you will have to pay this money back and that it could be a future burden.Borrow as little as possible with this type of loan.

When you graduate, you want your student loan to be as low as possible. Now that you have identified all your funding sources, and determined that you still need a loan, how do you decide how much you need? Here is a four-step approach:

Step 1:

Do an in-school budget, identifying your expenses (both education expenses and living expenses) and your resources (income, other contributions, and financial aid). Subtract your expenses from your resources. If there is a negative balance, you will need to borrow this amount. Your school can usually calculate the cost of attendance for the in-school period, which is typically less than 12 months. Think about how you will cover your expenses when you are not enrolled in classes.

Step 2:

To project your total student loan debt upon graduation, multiply the amount of assistance needed by the number of years you expect to be in school. Accrued interest will be added, which can significantly increase the total you will have to repay. Be sure that you understand how much you will be required to pay each month.

Step 3:

Estimate your expenses once you graduate. Your out-of-school budget will include most of the same components as your in-school budget, minus the education expenses. You will have new expenses related to your new job, as well as the added expense of your student loan payments. Estimate a monthly starting salary. Be conservative with these figures. Check with your school for more current information on average starting salaries for recent graduates.

Step 4:

Subtract your future expenses and anticipated monthly student loan payment from your future monthly income. If you have a surplus, it probably means that you can afford to borrow the amount you had planned. If you have a zero balance, it may mean that you have just enough to cover your future lifestyle. If you have a negative balance, you will need to reevaluate the amount you plan to borrow.

Another source of financial aid is your school itself. Speak with someone in your department who is knowledgeable about what aid is available and your realistic chances of getting it. Graduate school departments are accustomed to these requests. They realize financial considerations are a factor for most students. Be sure to ask about aid programs outside your own department. Many universities have these types of programs.

As you have read, the best form of graduate school aid is the fellowship. This is a cash award that does not need to be repaid. You do not have to work, either; it is simply a gift. Most fellowships are awarded by the university for an excellent academic record, but some are based on financial need. Fellowships can be for one to three years. Some can be renewed. The amount available varies widely. Some fellowships are only for a few hundred dollars, while others could cover the costs for your entire graduate school program, as well as a stipend for living expenses.

Do not limit yourself to fellowships available at your school. Many professional groups, government departments, and nonprofit organizations offer fellowships, although competition for these is steep. Most fellowship programs are not based on financial need, but rather a good GPA and test scores, your essays, and other application forms and recommendations.

Scholarships are also available. These are sometimes

based on student grades, which is often unfair. As we have discussed, undergraduate grades are often no predictor of performance in graduate school. Do not think that lesser grades will make you ineligible for scholarships. Some schools make a real effort to consider other factors and this is a growing trend.

Briefly

Noted

There are many scholarships available, and their selection process varies, so apply to as many as possible. There is no exact science to awarding scholarships, and capricious judgments are more often the rule than the exception.

Private and government scholarships have application deadlines at various times throughout the year. For some scholarships, the competition is open only to students who are already enrolled in graduate school; for other scholarships, you can apply before you are officially accepted into a program. Clearly, no award is given if you fail to get into graduate school. On the other hand, your chances of being accepted into almost any graduate program will increase considerably if you have been awarded a graduate scholarship from a government or private source. This is a good reason to take our advice to apply for as many scholarships as you can.

Many scholarships exist specifically for students studying in a certain field or for certain student populations such as ethnic minority groups. Many awards also have citizenship restrictions, and some must be awarded only within a student's home state. This is a vital piece of information because there is a fair chance that you will be choosing between graduate programs located in different states.

International students sometimes receive special consideration for waivers of tuition and other fees. An international student fee remission means the student is charged academic fees at the same rate as a student with domestic citizenship.

Still another form of financial aid is the assistantship. The main advantage they offer is that they are often generous, and they do not have to be paid back. Teaching assistants often teach classes of their own and get firsthand experience that might be valuable when they are job hunting. Many teaching assistants form friendships with their professors, which is often useful when they need recommendations or help finding a job after their graduation. Instead of teaching, research assistants work with computers or in labs, libraries, or other facilities. Do not think those are your only choices. In most graduate schools, students can become assistants in other departments such as administration. In most grad schools, assistants get tuition waivers or a stipend. To find out what is available, you can contact other students, read school catalogs and Web sites, or check with department heads.

The bottom line in financing your graduate school education is you can find some form of financial aid. It is only a matter of continuing to look until you are successful.

Locating Sources of Financial Aid

When it comes to finding funding for graduate school, what you do not know can harm you. For instance, did you know that many departments obtain their own pool of funds from private sources, alumni, grants, and other sources? These funds are often specified that they be used only for their students. How do you find out about them? Simply check with your advisor, dissertation chairperson, or other school officials.

Financial assistance programs come from a wide variety of sources. So where else do you look?

A source at the top of just about everyone's list is FinAid. This is a free site that was set up in 1994 as a public service by a financial-aid expert. FinAid has earned a stellar reputation as the best Web site of its kind, with everything you need to know about financial aid and a lot of advice and tools as well. It is informative, objective, and comprehensive.

Every major newspaper and personal finance magazine in the country has reviewed the site. The *New York Daily News* called FinAid "the hottest site on the Internet for financial aid tips." It is "the best place to begin a search," according to the *Chicago Sun-Times*, and "the grand-daddy of all Web sites," according to the *Boston Globe. Yahoo! Internet Life* said to "make FinAid your first stop. This site offers some of the best 'how to' guidance on securing financial aid." The site has won awards from the College Board, the National Association of Student Financial Aid Administrators, the National

Association of Graduate and Professional Students, and the American Institute for Public Service.

FinAid was created by Mark Kantrowitz, a financial-aid and college planning author who practices what he preaches: He managed to fund his own schooling without spending anything. The author of several books, he notes among his various achievements surviving a direct lightning strike on his home.

Fellowships and scholarships are more plentiful for graduate programs leading to a master's or Ph.D. in the sciences, engineering, the arts, and humanities. Such programs also may offer teaching and research assistantships that pay graduate school tuition or a stipend in exchange for teaching undergraduates or assisting in a research program. In contrast, graduate schools offering professional degrees in areas such as law, medicine, or business are more likely to expect you to rely on loans and your own resources. Some of the prestigious fellowships may be used toward programs of study leading to degrees or careers in any of these areas.

Many useful guides to graduate and professional study are available online. Be sure to talk to faculty in your field of interest. Seek out younger faculty members who may have had recent experiences in graduate school.

As you know by now, the best financial aid you can obtain is a fellowship (or two or more). While they are not exclusive to graduate students and can be awarded for a variety of other uses, graduate study in specific fields is often among the criteria for earning an award. The major advantage they have is that there is no repayment requirement. The amount of money varies widely, but it is common for these stipends to be anywhere from $10,000 to $25,000 for nine months to a year. They often include other benefits such as healthcare coverage.

Here are four tips for finding fellowships:

1. Do a keyword search on the Internet for "fellowship."

2. Network. Many fellowships are offered from the nonprofit community. There is great word-of-mouth information if you do your homework.

3. Identify nonprofit organizations of interest in your field, and contact them to see if they have fellowships.

4. Talk to current fellows. They expect to hear from others. Most fellowship Web sites profile current and former fellows. You might even find alumnus from your own campus.

Ivy League and top graduate schools (and others as well) often offer various free publications that include samples of winning fellowship proposals as well as other information. Harvard's *Scholarly Pursuits: A Practical Guide to Academe* offers advice and samples for academic career advancement.

Specialty areas ranging from bird-watching to microbiology are particularly good sources for fellowships. For example:

- The Program on Global Security and Cooperation at the Social Science Research Council offers a $19,000 a year stipend for Ph.D. students involved in peace, international cooperation, or security issues (**www.ssrc.org/programs/gsc**).

- The Michigan Space Grant Consortium offers research fellowships for graduate students in aerospace, space science, or mathematics with an award of $5,000 a year (**www.sprl.umich.edu**).

- The Smithsonian Institution Fellowship is available in various disciplines, including animal behavior, ecology, earth sciences, history of art, and the cultural history of the United States. Stipends are up to $22,000 a year (**www.si.edu/research+study**).

Other likely sources that will provide invaluable information about the entire spectrum of financial aid include the U.S. Department of Education, the Department of Health and Human Services, and the Department of Veterans Affairs. Educational institutions and private entities provide financial-aid funding. At the graduate level, you will sometimes have to be specific in your approach to finding information. For example, students pursuing a doctoral degree will find different funding sources than those pursuing a law degree. There is a general resource section at the end of this chapter.

You want to find out about resources that are related to your particular programs. For example, if you are in a scientific research course of study, you will want to rely heavily on a search engine for the Community of Science at **www.cos.com**. Here are some other scientific-based sources:

- American Association for the Advancement of Science Fellowships and Scholarships: **www. fellowships.aaas.org**

- American Association of University Women: **www.aauw.org/fga/fellowships_grants**

- American Psychological Association: **www.apa. org/students/funding.html**

- Environmental Protection Agency: **www.epa. gov/ocepa111/NNEMS**

- Hertz Foundation: **www.hertzfoundation.org/ awards.shtml**

- National Academies Fellowship Office: **www7. nationalacademies.org/fellowships**

- National Association for the Advancement of Colored People (NAACP): **www.naacp.org/ youth/scholarships/information**

- National Defense Science and Engineering Graduate Fellowships: **www.asee.org/ndseg**

- National Science Foundation: **www.nsf.gov**. Choose graduate students in the specialized information menu.

- Rotary International Ambassadorial Scholarships:**www.studyabroad.com/forum/rotary/rotary.html**

- U.S. Department of State (including the Fulbright Student Program): **http://exchanges.state.gov**

Minority groups often fare well with grants and fellowships. If you qualify, you might try sites such as the American Association of University Women at **www.aauw.org,** where there are a variety of stipends available. This association awards stipends of $5,000 to $12,000 to minority women who are graduate-degree candidates, and who are completing their final year of study in fields such as business administration and law.

Students who have not done well with federal funds, should check the various states at sites such as **www.gradview.com**. While some states primarily offer need-based financial aid, others offer merit-based financial aid to prospective students, generally with the requirement of a proven undergraduate record.

Many states have restrictions such as required research or travel, or only give awards to minority students.

Some states offer memorial scholarships to prospective graduate students. Sometimes, these programs offer a lower interest rate than federal loans for graduate students. In an effort to curb worker shortages, some states offer low or even non-interest graduate school loans as well as loan forgiveness programs for certain students in professions such as teaching, nursing, and healthcare. In exchange for getting a break on graduate school costs, students who take advantage of these are often required to pledge to work a certain number of years after graduation.

Students doing research on what types of financial aid are available often find that entrepreneurs in many cities have established scholarship search services. These services provide information about thousands of scholarships nationwide and are found in most major cities. The value of this information can vary considerably, so you should find out exactly what you are getting for your money.

Any student willing to invest time and effort is likely to be just as successful at locating funding sources as any fee-charging search service. Information about federal student aid programs is readily available at no charge, while college financial-aid offices are good sources for information as well. The reference section of a college library is likely to have guidebooks and directories listing grants and scholarships.

The Internet is a vast resource for finding information on financial aid. If you are pursuing a graduate degree for a particular profession, check to see if there is an affiliated organization Web site. University Web sites usually have this type of information. The best place to seek private scholarships or fellowships is usually through free online national databases and the department offices of the program you plan to pursue. Here is a list to get you started:

General Resources

- American Association of University Women: **www.aauw.org**

- Consumer Credit Counseling: **www.credit-counselingnwrqoek.org**

- FAFSA on the Web: **www.fafsa.ed.gov**

- FastWeb.com: **www. fastweb.com**

- Federal Student Aid Gateway: **www. studentaid.ed.gov**

- FinAid: **www.finaid.org**

- MBA Resources: **www.mba.com**

- National Association of Student Financial Aid: **www.studentair.org**

- NSLDS: **www.nslds.ed.gov**

- Peterson's: **www.petersons.com/graduate**

- Student Aid on the Web Scholarship Wizard: **studentaid2.ed.gov/getmoney/scholarship**

- U.S. Veterans Affairs Benefits: **www.va.gov**

Law school resources include the American Bar Association (**www.abanet.org**) and the Law School Admissions Council (**www.lsac.org**).

Medical, dental, and health professional resources include the Association of American Medical Colleges (**www.aamc.org**), the American Dental Association (**www. ada.org**), the American Physical Therapy Association (**www.apta.org**), and the U.S. Department of Health and Human Services (**www.hrsa.gov**).

Engineering resources include the National Society of Professional Engineers (**www.nspe.org**), the Society of Women Engineers (**www.swe.org**), and the National Council for Minorities in Engineering (**www.nacme.org**).

Provide are some reference books that will help you find available financial aid:

- *Free Money for Graduate School* by Laurie Blum

- *The College Blue Book: Scholarships, Fellowships, Grants and Loans,* includes graduate and postdoctoral awards from public and private sources. More than 3,500 award programs organized alphabetically in a general section and by discipline into 8 broad subject areas.

- *Financial Aid for the Disabled and Their Families* includes more than 1,500 scholarships, fellowships, loans, grant-in-aid awards, and awards for a complex range of disabilities.

- *The Foundation Directory* provides basic descriptions and current financial data for foundations "who were among the top 10,000 in terms of awards made in the last fiscal year." This resource is kept up-to-date with annual supplements.

- *The Foundation Directory, Part 2* is a supplement to the above and provides information on 10,000 second tier foundations.

- *The Grants Register* is intended primarily for students at the graduate level and for those requiring professional or advanced vocational training. Many of the awards are international in scope.

- *The Guide to Oregon Foundations* provides information on foundations residing in Oregon or with a history of giving in Oregon.

- *The Directory of Financial Aids for Women, 2005–2007,* includes five volumes of more than 5,000 entries listing scholarships, fellowships, loans, grants, awards, and internships for Native Americans, Hispanic Americans, African Americans, Asian Americans, and women.

- *Financial Aid for Research and Creative Activities Abroad, 2002–2004,* includes approximately 1,200 entries of funding opportunities for high school students, undergraduates, graduate students, post-doctoral students, and professionals. A wide range of activities is covered, from research to lectureships, and from exchange programs to creative projects.

- *Scholarships, Fellowships, and Loans* is a guide to more than 8,600 education-related, financial-aid programs for all levels of study, from undergraduate and vocational/technical programs to post-doctoral and professional study.

Who Gets Financial Aid and Who Does Not?

There is some debate about whether or not a doctorate degree is worth the time and trouble — not to mention the cost — but it is generally agreed that you will have a better chance of getting financial aid if you start as a doctoral candidate rather than a master's candidate. Usually, academic departments award more support to students who are in the Ph.D. program.

You typically do not apply for financial aid until you are accepted, so you probably want to do some research prior to that time. The published materials of most schools will usually have some general figures about what percentage of grad students receive financial aid. Sometimes, they will tell you the average aid package.

In grad school, a large percentage of financial aid comes in the form of two jobs — research assistants and teaching assistants. Getting one of these can be the difference between being able to attend or not, or the difference between a small or huge student debt load after graduation. Unfortunately, you usually will not know if you will be offered aid or how much until you have been accepted. A good solution is to visit the campus and talk with grad students in that department. You should be able to get a fairly good picture of what sort of financial-aid package a person with your grades and background can expect. Talk to a big enough cross section of students to form an intelligent opinion. You can also try calling the department directly — with a little luck, you will reach someone who is knowledgeable enough and helpful enough to look at your situation and give you an idea of what kind of aid you can expect.

If you do not get the aid you are hoping for, there is always the possibility of student loans and summer internships to help pay your way. Ultimately, you will have to do the math yourself to decide how much aid you will need.

Who gets financial aid and who does not can be a touchy subject because it all depends. Sometimes, what it depends on has nothing to do with income. Michael Fraher, director of financial aid at Vassar College, notes that more than one-third of the students there are getting need-based aid, even though the median family income for those receiving aid is a little more than $80,000.

Compared with undergraduate education, far less money

is available for grad school on the basis of financial need alone. You will find grad schools give away more awards based on merit than need. In a recent year, one in five graduate and professional students received a fellowship or grant — averaging $7,500 — with no strings attached. Students in the physical sciences, economics, engineering, religion, and theology have the best shot at getting a fellowship; fewer grants are available for advanced degrees in business and education. Assistantships, which require you to work in return for a stipend, are most common in the physical sciences. In a recent year, the average amount was $10,000.

Here are half a dozen suggestions on improving your chances of being the student who receives financial aid:

1. Start early. Decisions concerning fellowships, scholarships, and assistantships are often made at the department level. Awards for the academic year beginning each fall are determined within a month of the application deadline, generally the previous December or January, so it pays to start lobbying a year in advance.

2. If you are giving up a salary to attend graduate school, tell the school. The school may be sympathetic to your financial situation. Remember that the more the faculty wants you, the more aid you are likely to get.

3. Network. Seek out departments where you will be a good fit. You cannot underestimate the potential of throwing out a wide net.

4. A year or so before applying for grad school, e-mail scholars in programs of interest to you. They might be able to help you later when you apply for financial aid or a teaching job.

5. Go for a Ph.D. As you know, doctoral candidates have a better chance at receiving free money. If it makes sense in your field, apply for the advanced degree rather than a master's.

6. Look for financial help beyond the obvious. How about an outside company or organization that might benefit from your research? Contact them and volunteer your services.

All types of financial aid are far more available to full-time than part-time students. This is particularly true at the master's level; at the doctoral level, it is rare to find part-time students receiving any aid. Part-time students often have a source of aid not available to those studying full-time: employers. Students in education and social work often find their employer will reimburse at least part of their graduate school costs.

Various types of financial aids are tailored to specific groups of recipients. These categories include those who are of a certain race or ethnicity, those with disabilities, mature returning students, and students of a specific gender. A recent doctoral study found that minorities involved in doctoral study programs have an equal probability with non-minorities in receiving fellowships and grants. The same study found that students in pure fields such as science are more likely to receive financial aid than students studying the humanities and other liberal arts subjects.

In a doctoral program, your first and last years are usually the hardest times to get financial aid. Departments often want to see how you perform before they start paying you. Once you establish yourself, however, students find that there is a variety of financial aid, including assistantships. At the end of a doctoral program, the money tends to dry out, though at this time there are still various loans available.

When it comes to financial aid in graduate school, an important factor is your particular program. Financial-aid packages come in many varieties. In some fields, you are far more likely to get help than in other disciplines. Financial aid of all forms —whether it is federal or school loans or teaching assistantships — varies a great deal. There are no hard and fast rules, but here are some general guidelines for specific programs:

- Computer science. Your chances of getting loans are good at some technically oriented schools. At MIT, for example, scholarships comprise more than 80 percent of the financial aid that students receive.

- Education majors do not have a lot of choices for assistantships. Many students in this program find they need a combination of loans and other help.

- English is a popular program, but not a particularly high-paying one. A limited amount of fellowships are available, but teaching assistant positions are not typically available in the first year. Competition for the limited jobs is fierce.

- History offers some fellowships, and there is much competition for assistant positions. If you need money for a history program, you might be better off in the summer when there is more funding available.

- Psychology majors are better off than just about anyone else when it comes to finding teaching or research assistantships. In many schools, students accepted into Ph.D. programs can expect financial aid of some type.

- Students in the sciences fare far better than in any other area. Nearly half of all full-time candidates for master's degrees in science are paid for work as assistants. About three-quarters of science doctorate students receive assistantships, according to various sources.

The FAFSA is one of the most important documents you will fill out in your efforts at getting financial aid from the U.S. government. Completing this form will go a long way in determining if you qualify for financial aid. Here are ten tips to help you with this process:

1. Where do you find the paperwork? You can

find the FAFSA online, at high schools, at most libraries, or at a college financial-aid office.

2. The FAFSA lists a deadline of June 30, but your school's deadline may be sometime in early spring. Your best bet is to get it in as soon as possible after January 1.

3. If you do not yet have completed tax forms, estimate this information to the best of your ability. You will be able to make corrections later.

4. Even if you are applying to 12 schools, you need only complete one FAFSA. For aid at certain private schools, you may also have to submit the PROFILE, which is due in late September or early October. You can request that up to six schools receive your FAFSA information automatically.

5. In completing the form, always double check that your information is accurate and fill out the form completely. A failure to do so could lead to a costly delay in processing.

6. Be sure to submit all required forms along with your application. Check if your school requires any additional paperwork.

7. Meet every deadline. Even better, beat the deadline by as much as possible. Certain types of aid are offered on a first-come, first-served basis.

8. Applying online is the fastest way to submit your form and get results. To do so, you just need to request a PIN (Personal Identification Number) from **www.pin.ed.gov**. Filing online can help you catch errors right away.

9. Provide accurate information and make sure you understand everything you are signing.

10. If you have questions, many states have special call-in programs during January and February.

The best way to get financial aid is to try to connect with the professors and researchers who need graduate students. They will be the ones most eager to help you solve your financial challenges.

How to Make Sure You Get Financial Aid

For anyone who thinks financial aid for graduate students is hard to find, consider this statistic: there are 170,000 scholarships each year worth more than $1 billion. That does not count the value of assistantships or loans. Clearly, the money is there, but how can you be sure you are going to get some of it?

You can improve your chances with some patience and planning. Start looking at this critical aspect of graduate school at least a year before you are going. Below are some questions to ask yourself concerning your financial situation:

- How long does it normally take to complete your program?

- Will your financial aid be similar from year-to-year?

- Will you be able to work while you study?

- What are the application deadlines for admission and financial aid?

- Have you researched loan interest rates, repayment obligations, and tuition tax breaks?

Carefully filling out your financial aid forms is just as important as when you did your application papers for graduate school. When you send in your application for admission, you also apply for financial aid, either as part of the general application or on a separate form. A good application, with good references, transcripts, and a winning essay, can easily be worth $20,000 a year to you. A half-time assistantship may bring in $8,000 to $12,000, and tuition, except for in-state students at a public university, often exceeds $10,000.

Some universities will automatically consider you for all fellowships, scholarships, and assistantships when you submit your application for admission. At other universities the application for financial aid is a separate form. This point should be made clear in the instructions. If the request for financial aid is separate, be sure to fill it out even if you think you will not get the money. Be sure to check the date the application for financial aid is due. It may be different from the date for your application for admission.

Make sure your application is as good as you can possibly make it. Be meticulous. Even if your qualifications are good, if your application is mediocre you may get a notice that you are accepted with no offer of financial aid.

It might seem to you that assembling your financial plan is just as involved as preparing all the documents you needed to be accepted. You are absolutely correct. Here is a simple action timetable with specific goals to help you maximize your chances of aid:

Early Fall

Thoroughly research the funding opportunities available at your prospective programs and finalize your list of target schools. Research institutional funding possibilities. Do this ahead of time because many grant and fellowship programs have strict application deadlines.

Late Fall / Early Winter

If you are still in college, talk to professors in your discipline. They will be a source of recommendation letters later, which could help when applying for awards.

While interviewing and checking out campuses, take some time to meet with a financial-aid officer, as well as a dean in your field. They will know better than anyone about the best types of available aid.

Winter

Fill out the FAFSA, which is your passport to federal aid. Even if you do not plan to take a loan, fill it out. Circumstances can change. The FAFSA is required for any financial aid you may need in the future. Send it in as soon as possible after January 1 of the year you are applying. All grad students are considered independent for federal financial aid purposes.

Spring

Along with acceptance letters come financial-aid packages. Consider what is being offered to you and remember to take into account the available aid for the duration of your program, not just the first year. The best offer may not be the one with the highest first-year dollar value.

Summer

Prepare for the fall tuition bill by estimating the amount you will have to pay, comparing loan options, and talking to your school about tuition payment plans, if necessary.

If you are at the stage when you have been made a graduate school offer that includes financial aid, here are some questions you will want to ask:

- Is the award good for the entire time you will be in school?

- What obligations will you have in exchange for help?

- Will the award cover all your expenses?

If you get offered an assistantship as part of your financial package, you should find out:

- Does this also include paying your tuition?

- What is the work involved?

- Who will you be working with?

- If this is a teaching assistantship, will you be doing more than grading papers?

- If this is a research assistantship, what specific kinds of research will you be doing?

If you are financially strapped, a way to make some money with little effort is to become a Resident Assistant or RA. Back in college, you remember RAs as the people who kept the dorms in order. In some cases, they were graduate students who supervised a dormitory in exchange for tuition help. This option is primarily given to students studying psychology, counseling, and social work.

If you have problems matching your spending with your anticipated income, there are other avenues you might try. If you can show that you have financial need, you may be able to get a federal work-study job. Not every university has a work-study program, and some award these positions only to undergraduates, but many institutions include graduate students.

Up to 75 percent of the student's wages are paid by the federal work-study program. The department that employs you pays the rest. Because hiring for these positions is done by the department, people who get them usually work in areas related to their academic field, such as in university libraries, or laboratories, or assisting in summer recreation programs.

To get up-to-date information and to see if you are eligible, talk to the university's fellowship or financial aid office. Work-study positions may be controlled by the department or the graduate college, or some other entity within the university. You may have to search to find them, but it is certainly worth the effort.

Now That You Have Passed All Other Tests

Congratulations. You are in. Soon, you will start graduate school. Whether you are continuing your education right after college or returning to school after spending some time in the work force, this is going to be a major change in your life. Hopefully, you have thought about this for a long time because it is too late to change your mind now.

If you received a financial offer from your school, you should look it over one more time. Your offer should be in writing. A good first step at this point is to go over your finances one more time to see if you have made any mistakes.

Lifestyle decisions now pop up. Do you need a car? It would be a good way to economize if you can get by without it. Where are you going to live? You will probably want to be near your college, but housing there might cost more. Perhaps you need a car after all. These same issues will keep cropping up throughout your life as a graduate student.

Housing should not be a real problem since most colleges have a lot of options. College officials in charge of housing will have plenty of suggestions. While you are there, you might see the graduate advisor (GA). When school starts, the GA will be busy, but now is a quieter time when he or she can spend some time with you. You should leave the office with a good idea of the courses you will be taking.

Just before school starts, there should be an orientation program for new students. Your own department should also have some type of learning session as well.

Consider becoming a student assistant. Even if you do not need the money, the job is an education in itself. It shows that you are a serious student, and it will help you meet others in your department. At some point, you may need references, which should not come from someone who only recognizes you in class and knows little more than your name. Ideally, references come from professors who have seen your work and gotten to know your personality. Becoming a student assistant will give you the opportunity to cultivate these relationships.

You will probably have a fairly definite schedule of classes, which you will need to make some basic decisions about. Make sure the classes that you choose are not only helpful to your end goals, but are also of interest to you personally. Sometime early in the school year, pencil in a tentative schedule of courses, examinations, and thesis requirements. This will give you an idea of what you will be facing in the future.

Getting to know the faculty should be among your goals. Some professors will be more friendly and approachable than others, but there are numerous social occasions when you will have a chance to meet and talk informally with your teachers. This is not only instructive in its own right, but most students find this type of interaction interesting and enjoyable.

If your school has a graduate student association, it is a good idea to check it out. Not all of these groups are helpful and some, in fact, are a waste of time. At the very least, they often can be a good place to meet other students.

If you are a teaching assistant and do not come from a teaching background, you will have an entire new skill to master. Teaching college students is different from teaching younger students. As a teaching assistant, you will probably do more than grade papers, and you will almost certainly spend some time in the classroom. Carefully prepare for any lectures and classroom work you do. One of the hardest things in the world is to face a classroom of students with nothing to say when you have nothing for them to do.

Both in and out of the classroom, you are going to be making a lot of first impressions. No matter how large your university, you will be a part of a much smaller group. You will be noticed. Your work will be scrutinized. You might want to keep that in mind as soon as you arrive on campus.

After you settle into your routine, your goal is to complete graduate school, but you should also aim to do more than get good grades. No gentlemanly Cs are acceptable here. You need to get As with an occasional B if you have a good excuse.

Some students find graduate school overwhelming. They have trouble doing the work or do not have enough time to complete their course requirements. If this happens to you, try talking to your professors or other students to get some suggestions for improvement. Remember that you went through a lot of effort to get where you are, and you want to do everything you can to make your graduate years successful ones. Do not procrastinate. Deal with problems immediately.

The same applies to money problems. It is not uncommon for grad students to find that, despite all their planning, they do not have enough money to pay their bills. Perhaps they have a family and a family member incurred serious medical bills, or maybe they have a spouse who lost his or her job. All kinds of situations can come up to throw a monkey wrench into the best laid plans. If this happens to you, you can always look around for extra loans, or see if a sympathetic relative will give you some money to be paid back later, or find some other way to add to your income.

You will get a lot of offers for credit cards and for "easy" loans. Be careful. Remember that educational loans are all right, but credit card debt is not.

One area you might not have thought about if you are young is health insurance. Some universities require students to pay for a school-wide health plan. Some plans are good, while others are not. If you have an option on insurance, you will probably want to buy it through the university. Going to private industry for insurance is often prohibitively expensive, even if you are a young man or woman in good health.

For many students, choosing a thesis director or advisor is almost as important as choosing health insurance. This choice is particularly critical if you are going for a doctorate. When you start school as an undergraduate, you are generally assigned an advisor, but this is an entirely different relationship. You will have a close association for years with your grad school advisor. You want someone who is interested in you and your progress, and will help you throughout your education.

Another area that may cause you concern will be tests. There are a lot of them in graduate school, and you will have to become familiar with a lot of material to prepare for them. You are not an unusual or neurotic person if this prospect makes your stomach flutter, at least a little. The best thing is to head off panic before it starts. Your first step is to learn to relax. Read books or listen to tapes for soothing advice, such as calming breathing exercises, if test anxiety is among your concerns. One way to avoid panic during an exam is simple preparation. Do your homework. This should give you the confidence you need to calmly face the tests.

Briefly Noted

Many departments have administrative secretaries. It is a good idea to get to know him or her because they often know everything that is going on. They can help solve any problems that come up. They are usually willing to go out of their way to help you in whatever you need.

Many undergraduates seem to think that cheating is no big deal. Many of them manage to get away with it. Do not even think about cheating in graduate school. If you are caught copying an exam or turning in someone else's work, you will likely be kicked out of school. Your career will be over before it even starts.

Graduate school may be particularly difficult for people who have been out of college for several years. They have to make even more of an adjustment than others. They may be uprooting their circle of friends and family to move to another area to attend school. They may have an immediate family with a wife and children to worry about. But keep in mind that this kind of student also has some advantages. He or she is more mature. They have learned to budget their time. They are often more patient.

Briefly

Woody Allen says that "90 percent of life is showing up."

Noted

Whatever your situation as a student, you should take the attitude that if there are problems — and everyone has them, no matter what they do — there are also solutions. Remember how you got this far and that memory should help move you through any difficulties you encounter.

Rating Graduate Schools and Resources

Have you ever heard of the Moore School at the University of South Carolina? Perhaps not, but it was rated among the top graduate programs in the country for 18 consecutive years by the respected *U.S. News & World Report*. Of course, that rating was in the category of *international business*.

This brings up the problem inherent in rating the top graduate schools. It depends on what discipline you are talking about. Does the school specializes in international business, engineering, or nursing?

Certainly Ivy Leagues institutions such as Harvard, Columbia, and Princeton get high ratings. But ratings do not always tell you what you need to know. Choosing a graduate school solely by its rankings is never recommended. This can be a confusing process, but by doing independent comparisons, students can choose what school best fits their own needs. Here are half a dozen key factors to take into consideration when comparing graduate school ratings:

1. What are your priorities? Graduate schools cover a wide spectrum in their specialties. If you are majoring in English literature, MIT is not going to be your best choice, despite its sterling reputation. Consider using various rankings.

2. Look at the ranking criteria. Different criteria are used by various ranking sources. One area to look closely at is student-to-faculty ratio. Some ranking services view this as an important reason for their position. You also want to look at employment success after graduation. This is a good indication of a school's overall quality.

3. As the old saying goes, "consider the source." If you are interested in one or another program, engineering for example, find out what national associations have to say about which schools have outstanding graduate programs in that field.

4. Colleges and universities are often sorted into tiers. This system can be misleading. If a so-called second- or third-tier university has an amazing computer program, it might appear low on an overall ranking list. But if your interest is in computers, it may be

the perfect school for you. Look for specific rankings in areas of your interest rather than overall ratings.

5. Because you have to be financially savvy when deciding on grad school, take a close look at reputation and cost. Harvard has a great name, but it is expensive. Do you need to spend that money to get into an Ivy League or top school? Perhaps a lesser-known school that costs less and has a fantastic program in your field would be a better choice.

6. Big-name research universities almost always show up at the top in national rankings. That is a long tradition in rankings and some schools are merely coasting. If you are not interested in a research program, do you need the school's reputation? If you are studying English, for example, a better choice might be found elsewhere.

If you do not need to go to Harvard to reach your educational and professional goals, browse the rankings accordingly. If your long-term goals, monetary resources, or educational background do not match up with those schools, browse different rankings. Consider rankings of smaller institutions or more affordable and accessible ones.

With that in mind, here is what *U.S. News & World Report* ranked as among the best schools for 2008:

Top Business Graduate Schools

- Harvard University

- Stanford University

- University of Pennsylvania (Wharton)

- Massachusetts Institute of Technology (Sloan)

- Northwestern University (Kellogg)

Top Law Graduate Schools

- Yale University

- Harvard University

- Stanford University

- New York University

- Columbia University

Top Medical Graduate Schools (Research)

- Harvard University

- Johns Hopkins University

- University of Pennsylvania

- Washington University in St. Louis

- University of California — San Francisco

Top Engineering Schools

- Massachusetts Institute of Technology

- Stanford University

- University of California — Berkeley

- Georgia Institute of Technology

- University of Illinois — Urbana–Champaign

Other Resources for Graduate Study

www.gradschools.com

www.graduateguide.com

www.gradprofiles.com

American Association of University Women: **www.aauw. org**

Association for Support of Graduate Students: **www. asgs.org**

National Association of Graduate/Professional Students: **www.nagps.org**

www.acinet.org

www.bls.gov

www.jobstar.org

Sources of Financial Aid

Financial aid: **www.finaid.org**

FastWEB: **www.fastWEB.com**

College Board Scholarship Search: **www.collegeboard. org**

CollegeNet Mach 25: **www.collegenet.com**

Scholarship Resource Network Express: **www.srnexpress. com**

National Science Foundation: **www.nsf.gov**

U.S .Department of Education: **www. ed.gov/about/ pubs/intro/index**

U.S. Department of Education: Federal Student Aid: **www. studentaid.ed.gov**

Mellon Fellowships: **www.woodrow.org/mellon**

The Rhodes Scholarship Trust: **www.rhodesscholar. org**

Sallie Mae College Answer: **www.collegeanswer.com**

For Minorities

The Black Collegian Online: **www.black-collegian.com**

Black Issues in Higher Education: **www.blackissues.com**

United Negro College Fund: **www.uncf.org**

National Black Graduate Association: **www.nbgsa.org**

For Disabled Applicants

Testing information: **www.etc.org/disability/index**

Accommodations: **www. health.gwu.edu**

Conclusion

The first issue you face in graduate school is to decide if it is worth the time, trouble, and money it will require. A second decision is whether to go right after you have finished your undergraduate degree, or to wait until you have spent a few years, or even longer, in the job market.

Once you decide on graduate school, you must face up to the fact that getting into any graduate school is difficult enough, but being accepted by the best and the Ivy League schools is even harder.

There are shortcuts, however, and ways to ensure your best chances for acceptance. If you learn to excel at every requirement for acceptance — such as writing the best essays, maximizing your test performances, and selecting people to write outstanding letters of recommendation, among other tasks — you are well on your way to increasing your chances of getting in. It is not an easy goal, but with a little help, you will be surprised at the many ways you can overcome all the hurdles before you. In the end, you will almost certainly find that the effort has been worth it.

Bibliography

Books that are useful in getting into the top graduate schools:

America's Best Graduate Schools. Published annually by *U.S. News & World Report,* Washington, DC, 2008.

Financing Graduate School: How to Get the Money You Need for Your Graduate School Education, 2nd edition, Patricia McWade. Lawrenceville, NJ: Peterson's, 1996.

How to Write a Winning Personal Statement for Graduate and Professional School, 3rd edition, Richard J. Stelzer. Lawrenceville, NJ: Petersons, 1993.

Peterson's Guide to Graduate and Professional Programs, Vols. 1–6, published annually by Peterson's, Lawrenceville, NJ. An enormous set of volumes that provides information on virtually all graduate programs.

Sweaty Palms: The Neglected Art of Being Interviewed, H. Anthony Medley. Rev. ed. New York, NY: Hachette Book Group, 2005.

The Complete Scholarship Book 2nd edition. Student Services, Inc., 1997.

Author Biography

David Wilkening is a former newspaperman (Chicago, Washington, and Detroit) who has been a freelance writer for more than two decades. He specializes in travel and business writing. Years after he earned his bachelor's degree, he went back to school to get a master's degree. His purpose was to teach college, and he does that today as an adjunct journalism professor at the University of Central Florida. Unfortunately, he did not take his own advice about financing graduate school.

Index